COMPARE
ISAIAH

FRANCES:
WHAT A GREAT LADY AND A GREAT
FRIEND TO MY FOLKS. THANKS FOR YOUR
INTEREST IN THIS BOOK. I HOPE IT IS
ENLIGHTENING

Mark Stewart

COMPARE
ISAIAH

UNDERSTANDING
BIBLICAL SCRIPTURES
IN THE
BOOK OF MORMON

Mark Swint

Horizon
Springville, Utah

ISBN 13: 978-0-88290-960-8

Published by Horizon Publishers, an imprint of Cedar Fort, Inc.
2373 W. 700 S., Springville, UT 84663
Distributed by Cedar Fort, Inc., www.cedarfort.com

LIBRARY OF CONGRESS CATALOGING-IN-PUBLICATION DATA

Swint, Mark, 1951-
    Compare Isaiah : understanding biblical Scriptures in the Book of Mormon / Mark Swint.
        p. cm.
    Summary: A study of the verses from the Book of Isaiah and other biblical writings found in the Book of Mormon.
    Includes bibliographical references and index.
    ISBN 978-0-88290-960-8 (alk. paper)
    1. Bible. O.T. Isaiah--Quotations in the Book of Mormon. 2. Book of Mormon--Criticism, interpretation, etc. I. Title.

    BX8627.S94 2009
    289.3'22--dc22
                                        2008048131

Cover design by Angela Olsen
Cover design © 2009 by Lyle Mortimer
Edited and typeset by Melissa J. Caldwell

Printed in the United States of America

10 9 8 7 6 5 4 3 2 1

Printed on acid-free paper

To my son Daniel,
whose faithfulness and willingness
to serve his Heavenly Father
was my inspiration to write this book.

Contents

Introduction ix

1. Not a Hundredth Part 1

2. 1 Nephi Text 9

3. Jacob's Isaiah 31

4. Nephi's Isaiah—The Warning 41

5. Nephi's Isaiah—The Hope 65

6. "A Book that is Sealed" 83

7. Abinadi and King Noah 99

8. The Savior's Visit to the Americas 115

9. The Words of Malachi 127

10. The Sermon on the Mount 145

About the Author 164

INTRODUCTION

Though they serve vastly different religions and cultures of the world, almost all books of scripture share certain areas of commonality. For example, almost all sacred ancient writings contain a version of the story of the great flood. Many books offer similar accounts of the creation of this earth and its inhabitants. Almost all have Adam and Eve figures as well as a war in heaven scenario. They may adapt the names and particular details to more comfortably fit their ethnic or nationalistic identities, and certainly, over time, some stories take on a purely local setting, but the essence of the stories conveys the same message.

The books of scripture for the three great religious movements of Judaism, Islam, and Christianity share an even closer bond. The Torah, Koran, and Bible are products of people known as "Shemites" or descendants of Shem, the most blessed of Noah's three sons. Known as the "Great High Priest," Shem had many descendants, who are now known as "Semites," and they include such great people as the Arabs, Hebrews, Phoenicians, Syrians, Assyrians, and Babylonians. It would stand to reason that if these people did indeed share a common ancestry, they would also share a related history. And so it is that the early patriarchs from Adam through Noah and on to Abraham appear in one form or another in their scriptures. Abraham, in particular, figures prominently in all three aforementioned books, as it was through his sons Isaac and Ishmael that the Arab nations and the Hebrews evolved. Not only do the Torah, Koran, and Old Testament all recognize these figures, but so, also, do the vast majority of ancient documents, which have come to light in the last 150 years of archeological exploration in the Middle East. We now have, for example, "Enoch" texts from Ethiopia, Greece, the Slavic regions, Syria, and also from the Hebrews, and more recently, the Dead Sea Scrolls, as well as our own Joseph Smith "Enoch" text as found in Moses 6 and 7 in the Pearl of Great Price. While details vary, the underlying theme remains constant among them all.

It should come as no surprise, therefore, that the Book of Mormon also contains references to these same people. The details it provides illuminate rather than confuse the already expansive body of scripture extant in the world.

What is surprising and unique about the Book of Mormon is that it is the only book of scripture that directly quotes passages from another book of scripture. Within the pages of the Book of Mormon we find twenty-six chapters of Isaiah, three chapters of Matthew, and two chapters of Malachi cited in their entirety (some might call this plagiarism; however, the quotes are fully attributed to their original authors). This citing of a more ancient scripture firmly and unequivocally ties the Book of Mormon to the people of the Old Testament and establishes a bond between the two civilizations.

The way we, as students of the Book of Mormon, recognize these passages is very easy; each chapter so cited begins with "Compare Isaiah . . ." The first example is found in 1 Nephi 20 in which we are instructed to "Compare Isaiah 48." All too often we are tempted to skip over these chapters because they're "not really Book of Mormon history" and, after all, isn't that what we are studying? Those who do go ahead and read the Isaiah passages often do so for the sake of saying they have read every word of the Book of Mormon. However, seldom do we lay open the Bible side by side with the Book of Mormon and actually do as the chapter heading directs: compare the two. This is unfortunate for, contrary to popular belief, the Isaiah, Malachi, and Matthew passages are not copied verbatim from one or another version of the Bible! Joseph Smith did not skip over these passages nor did he take the text from the Bible as an easy way around the difficult process of translating. Rather, he continued doing what he had been doing, that is, he translated every word from the golden plates as it came to him. As a result, though the passages are remarkably similar, they nevertheless show unique and sometimes crucial differences.

I have found studying these differences to be most educational and enlightening, and it is my hope, in the following pages, to bring to life, for the reader, a portion of the Book of Mormon that has all too often lain hidden in plain sight while at the same time clarifying why even the Savior said, "Great are the words of Isaiah."

1

NOT A HUNDREDTH PART

As the Book of Mormon begins, Nephi declares to us that he is writing his record according to "the learning of the Jews and the language of the Egyptians" (1 Nephi 1:2). Latter day scholars tell us that the "Reformed Egyptian" used by Nephi was probably a form now known as Meroitic Egyptian[1] which was essentially a type of shorthand developed by Egyptians in the seventh century BC and used throughout their kingdom (which at that time included Jerusalem). Discoveries made since the publication of the Book of Mormon reveal that regular Egyptian is significantly more efficient to write than Hebrew, and the Meroitic shorthand, developed far up the Nile, was even more compact and easy to work with than Egyptian. It would make sense that Nephi, and the prophets who followed him, would seek the most efficient method of writing as they all noted the great difficulty they faced as they struggled to adequately write their history.

> And now, behold, we have written this record according to our knowledge, in the characters which are called among us reformed Egyptian, being handed down and altered by us according to our manner of speech.
>
> And if our plates had been sufficiently large we should have written in Hebrew; but the Hebrew hath been altered by us also; and if we could have written in Hebrew, behold ye would have no imperfection in our record. (Moroni 9:32–33)

Limited space on the plates and difficulty in writing required that only the most important information be written down. Nephi expressed this almost immediately in his record:

> Wherefore, I shall give commandment unto my seed, that they shall not occupy these plates with things which are not of worth unto the children of men. (1 Nephi 6:6)

Mormon, likewise, states;

> And now there cannot be written in this book even a hundredth part of the things which Jesus did truly teach unto the people. (1 Nephi 26:6)

Jacob and Moroni also express the difficulty with which they struggled to record the works of their people. It stands to reason, therefore, that no extraneous or superfluous words should ever occupy the pages of the Book of Mormon, and yet, within the first one hundred pages we have no less than twenty-five pages devoted to quoting Isaiah. This seems grossly inefficient and redundant. After all, the Nephites had most of the portions of the Old Testament up to Jeremiah with them as they trekked across the desert and across the sea to their new home on the American continents. Why then would Book of Mormon authors commit so much effort and valuable space to words already recorded and available on other documents? Perhaps the best way to answer that question is to learn why they were valuable to the people in the first place.

It is not insignificant that the first real story of the Book of Mormon concerns the efforts of Nephi and his brothers to acquire, from Laban, the plates of brass, which contained a record of the genealogy of their forefathers and a history of the Jews. This record was apparently so valuable to Lehi's family that Nephi and his brothers risked their lives and all of their family fortune to secure it. Eventually, Nephi was moved upon by the Spirit to slay Laban in order to get the records, for as the Spirit told him:

> Behold the Lord slayeth the wicked to bring forth his righteous purposes. It is better that one man should perish than that a nation should dwindle and perish in unbelief. (1 Nephi 4:13)

The Lord knew that entire cultures could perish without records that would transmit their history, genealogy, and perhaps most important, a knowledge of the covenants and the law, as given to their fathers. We see evidence of this early in the Book of Mormon as we read the sad tale of the Mulekites[2] who left Jerusalem shortly after Lehi's group. They did not bring with them any records, and in a very few generations, they had lost all connection with their ancestors, their cultural roots, and even their language! The value of the records that Nephi and his brothers recovered reveals itself when Nephi teaches his people from these same ancient scriptures. He begins by teaching the words of all the ancient prophets concerning the doings of the Lord with regard to his people, while at the same time foreshadowing the importance of the Book of Mormon to our own generation today. He states:

> Now it came to pass that I, Nephi, did teach my brethren these things; and it came to pass that I did read many things to them, which were engraven upon the plates of brass, **that they might know concerning the doings of the Lord in other lands, among people of old**. (1 Nephi 19:22; emphasis added)

If ancient records of people in other lands were of great value to the Nephites, it stands to reason that the records of the Nephites, though they be other people in other times and in other lands, might be of great worth to us. Nephi shows the way this is accomplished as he continues.

> But that I might more fully persuade them to believe in the Lord their Redeemer I did read unto them that which was written by the prophet Isaiah; for I did liken all scriptures unto us, that it might be for our profit and learning. (1 Nephi 19:23)

Nephi clearly understood that the value of scriptures was in their applicability to the times and circumstances of those who heard or read them rather than in their purely historical content. It only follows that he used that criteria to decide what accounts and teachings he would include in his own records. While he undoubtedly read many more old scriptures to his people than those recorded, he only wrote words that could be likened to the days and circumstances of the people who would read his account. One thousand years later Mormon would imply the very same thing as he compiled and abridged the massive quantity of records that fell under his stewardship. This same practice of likening the words of old prophets to contemporary times was used in Jerusalem as well. In Romans 15 we read Paul's words concerning the words of earlier prophets:

> For whatsoever things were written aforetime were written for our learning, that we through patience and comfort of the scriptures might have hope. (v. 4)

As Mormon made his narrative it must be remembered that no Nephite eyes would ever see the words he painstakingly engraved on the golden plates. All his statements, pleas, and admonitions were directed particularly and solely to us in these latter days. The title page of the Book of Mormon declares that he wrote his abridgement under commandment from the Lord by the spirit of prophecy and revelation. While we don't have a specific account of that revelation or commandment, we can get a good idea of what transpired by reading Moroni's account of his own revelation on the subject:

> Behold, I speak unto you as if you were present, and yet ye are not. But behold, Jesus Christ hath shown you unto me, and I know your doing. (Mormon 8:35)

By showing both Mormon and Moroni our day, they were able to more wisely mold their records and writings to address our particular needs. Moroni makes a humble plea for our patience and declares that he knows the value of sharing their weaknesses and imperfections with us so that we might learn wisdom. He states:

> Behold, I speak unto you as though I spake from the dead; for I know that ye shall have my words. Condemn me not because of mine imperfection, neither my father, because of his imperfection, neither them who have written before him; but rather give thanks unto God that he hath made manifest unto you our imperfections, that ye may learn to be more wise than we have been. (Mormon 9:30–31)

How somber it must have been for men like Nephi, Mormon, and Moroni to ponder the visions they saw of our day and attempt to engrave, on metal plates, fitting words of warning and caution that we might possibly avoid the very things that brought down their people. All these things only reinforce the notion that nothing was going onto the plates save it had great value to the people of our own generation here in the latter days. This gives all the more reason to marvel that fully one quarter of the early pages of their record are devoted exclusively to the words of Isaiah.

Why Isaiah?

While many other prophets (Zenos, Zenock, and Neum, to name a few) are referenced by Book of Mormon authors, it is Isaiah who is first quoted verbatim in an entire chapter. In fact, Isaiah is the source of over

85 percent of the biblical scriptures in the Book of Mormon. To understand why this is so requires an examination of who the man Isaiah was, as well as an understanding of his mission.

In citing Isaiah more than any other biblical prophet, the Book of Mormon is only following the example of the New Testament. Researchers and scholars who study such things have found that Isaiah is the most quoted biblical prophet in the scriptures. He is quoted more often than Paul, Peter, or John. Remarkably, he is even quoted more than Jesus! In the account of the Savior's visit to the Nephites we see an occasion where Jesus quotes the entire 54th chapter of Isaiah and then expounds upon it to the people and gives them the following endorsement and charge:

> And now, behold, I say unto you, that ye ought to search these things. Yea, a commandment I give unto you that ye search these things diligently; for great are the words of Isaiah. (3 Nephi 23:1)

Isaiah was a prophet in Jerusalem from 740–701 BC, a period of forty years, during which time he served as the chief advisor to King Hezekiah. This put him about a hundred years before Nephi, which means he was to Nephi as Lorenzo Snow would be to us today. In other words, he was a "modern" prophet in Nephi's day. It can be reasonably assumed that his words were relatively fresh and accessible to the people of 600 BC.

Certainly, most biblical prophets taught of the coming Messiah. However, many focused their particular ministries on the specific events of their day. Often they would foresee victory over a certain enemy or constantly remind the people of the sanctity of the law of Moses. Many times Old Testament prophets dealt with issues specific to the House of Israel and the turmoil within it at that time. It seems the preservation of the tribes of Israel in olden times was a primary focus. Just keeping the House of Israel together was a full time (and ultimately futile) job.

A close scrutiny of Isaiah's teachings shows that his mission was more far reaching than most other prophets'. Isaiah seems to have been a sort of Old Testament John the Baptist. That is, he acted as a herald for the coming Savior. The angelic messenger who proclaimed the Savior's birth seemed to be quoting Isaiah 9 when he declared "for unto you is born this day, in the city of David, a Savior which is Christ the Lord" (Luke 2:11; compare Isaiah 9:6). Likewise, when Moroni appeared to Joseph Smith in September 1823, he quoted from the eleventh chapter of Isaiah and proclaimed that the time was at hand for his words to be fulfilled.

The majority of Isaiah's teaching fell into two categories. The first category dealt with everything about the Savior and his mission to the house of Israel and to the world. He joyed in foretelling the coming of the Savior both as a mortal at the meridian of time and the glorious God of Israel returning at the last day. Many of Isaiah's prophecies reveal the events that will ultimately lead to the Savior's return and he clearly shows the state of the people who will receive him. In conjunction with his prophesies about the fate of the house of Israel, Isaiah foretold the coming forth of the Book of Mormon. It was he who prophesied that the Nephites would be destroyed, and that their record would come forth out of the ground in the form of a sealed book:

> And thou shalt be brought down, and shall speak out of the ground, and thy speech shall be low out of the dust, and thy voice shall be, as of one that hath a familiar spirit, out of the ground, and thy speech shall whisper out of the dust. . . .
>
> And the vision of all is become unto you as the words of a book that is sealed, which men deliver to one that is learned, saying, Read this, I pray thee: and he saith, I cannot, for it is sealed:
>
> And the book is delivered to him that is not learned, Saying, Read this I pray thee: and he saith I am not learned. (Isaiah 29:4, 11–12)

Isaiah also had a very specific message, which became a recurring theme throughout his entire ministry. He constantly taught that God requires righteousness from his people and unless they obey him they will be smitten and scattered by their enemies and will be brought down as far as is necessary, until they are humbled. The Lord will do this because righteousness is required for those who will stand in his presence at the last day. This part of his ministry was simple and straightforward— "and inasmuch as ye shall keep my commandments, ye shall prosper" (1 Nephi 2:20).

Isaiah taught according to the manner of speech common to Semitic people in which all messages were a balance of positive and negative messages. All Isaiah's warnings and admonitions were balanced by a message of hope which, in the case of the Israelites, was that in the last days Israel will be restored and established in the land of their inheritance and the Lord will dwell in the midst of his people, who will be called Zion.

This Messianic thrust in Isaiah's teachings, along with his obvious familiarity with the coming forth of the Book of Mormon, makes him the ideal source for Nephi and subsequent Book of Mormon prophets to quote. As justification for quoting Isaiah, Nephi stated that the Lord:

> Did show unto the prophets of old all things concerning them; and also he did show unto many concerning us; wherefore, it must needs be that we know concerning them for they are written upon the plates of brass. (1 Nephi 19:21)

Nephi proceeds to once again exhort the people to consider the words of the prophets, including Isaiah, and liken them unto themselves. This is a recurring theme for Nephi in particular, as he seems to have a clear vision of how prophetic words are universal in their applicability. It is only logical that Nephi would feel this way and that this would have been a primary motivator for him in keeping his own record. It must be recognized, and constantly remembered by any student of the Book of Mormon, that the prophets who made this record knew that their voices would "whisper out of the dust." It is interesting that they used the metaphor of dust rather than saying, "Our voices ring out from the past," or "Our voices declare with the sound of trumpets through the ages." No such bold expression was used. Rather, they acknowledged that their people would be brought down, in humility, to the dust. Neither would their voices ring loud and clear but rather, they would "whisper." We must have compassion for such men, who knew that their mission to save their own people would ultimately fail but who saw, in the future, another audience who might, through the sad accounts in the Book of Mormon, learn the lessons therein and save their own generation.

As latter-day possessors and caretakers of the Book of Mormon, we must constantly remind ourselves that there is nothing joyful about the Book of Mormon. It is a sad tale of a fallen people whose cycles of righteousness and wickedness ultimately led to their complete and utter destruction. Its people cry unto us saying, "Do not do as we have done. Learn from our mistakes and save yourselves!"

It is remarkable to note how closely the prophecies of Isaiah parallel the hopes that all the Nephite prophets held for their people. Well before Lehi left Jerusalem, the House of Israel had been split into two different kingdoms. The one we know as the Lost Ten Tribes is commonly called the kingdom of Israel and was lost to the common knowledge of man almost immediately. The other, called the kingdom of Judah, was comprised of the tribe of Judah and a smattering of remnants from the other tribes, including Joseph, who remained in Jerusalem and the land of Judea. They were destined to be driven from their homes and scattered to the winds. Indeed, this was the reason Lehi fled with his family into the desert in the first place. As the various Book of Mormon prophets recorded their history, they recognized that the splitting of their family into the Nephites and the Lamanites was symbolic of the House of Israel. It follows then that the words of Isaiah would have been powerful reminders of the fate and the responsibilities that awaited them. No other Old Testament prophet had so concisely spoken to their condition as had Isaiah. It is no wonder that he was their strongest link to their ancestral home and the larger family of Israel. As we come to understand this, we see more clearly why Isaiah's words are so abundantly provided throughout the Book of Mormon.

Notes

1. Hugh Nibley, *Teachings of the Book of Mormon—Semester 1* (Salt Lake City: Covenant Communications, 2004).
2. Mulek was the sole surviving son of King Zedekiah.

2

1 NEPHI TEXT

There are seven groups of Biblical texts in the Book of Mormon. Five are from Isaiah, one is from Malachi, and one is from Matthew. The Isaiah texts appear first and continue to appear until the Savior draws from Malachi and Matthew during his visit to the Nephites after his crucifixion and resurrection. Isaiah's words appear in 1 Nephi, 2 Nephi (two groups), Mosiah, and 3 Nephi.

The key to understanding the words of Isaiah, at least as they appear in the Book of Mormon, is to study the circumstances of the people to whom they were delivered. When we understand what issues the people were dealing with, or perhaps more correctly, what issues the prophets had to deal with concerning the people, we begin to comprehend what message would be most beneficial to them. We must remember that the prophets who quoted Isaiah felt his words were applicable to their particular times and circumstances and could be "likened unto us." By understanding the problems facing them, we could, with a little effort, probably predict which sections of Isaiah could best be likened unto Nephi's people.

Nephi's mission was arduous from the start. He, like his brothers, faced the complete disruption of the life he had theretofore known. However, unlike his more obstinate brothers Laman and Lemuel, he accepted the coming changes with faith and steadfastness. He had faith in his father and faith in his Lord. Yet, sadly, during the twenty or so years[1] after they left Jerusalem, Nephi faced an almost constant display of faithlessness and disenchantment from many of his people. He had witnessed his own brothers being visited and ministered to by angels only to see them commence murmuring immediately afterwards. He miraculously built a sturdy sailing vessel while enduring the mocking derision of those who were certain he was crazy. He saw the Liahona fail when his people bound him up and tied him to a mast in the middle of the voyage across the Pacific. Over and over again, Nephi's people witnessed the mercy of the Lord each time they repented and, over and over again, they saw things go badly when they turned away from righteousness and forgot the Lord. Nephi was frustrated that they could not seem to understand the connection between righteousness and prosperity, nor that between wickedness and travail.

Nephi's challenge was exacerbated by his dual role as both the spiritual and political leader of the people. While he presumably had the support of those who viewed him as a prophet, he also faced the opposition of those who resented his political leadership over them. As a result, his own credibility was lacking among a portion of the people. It is understandable then that Nephi turned to the words of Isaiah, words spoken, seemingly directly, to his people. He said:

> Wherefore I spake unto them saying: Hear ye the words of the prophet, ye who are a remnant of the House of Israel, a branch who have been broken off; hear ye the words of the prophet which were written unto the house of Israel, and liken them unto yourselves. (1 Nephi 19:24)

Isaiah's Words

The first group of scriptures quoted by Nephi is from Isaiah 48 and 49 and appears in the Book of Mormon as 1 Nephi 20 and 21. As we take a close look at Isaiah's words, we will see that the message of this particular passage is about Israel's obstinance in acknowledging God as their Lord and the resulting consequences. Isaiah reveals the near future as he correctly foresees the Babylonian captivity of Israel. However, consistent with the Semitic manner of speaking, his prophecy also contains words of hope to balance the admonition. He promises that Israel will rise again in the last days and he goes on to explain that all the forthcoming travail could be avoided if they would simply give heed to the words of the prophets. He is clear about the fact that God requires righteousness.

This is Nephi's message also: with wickedness comes adversity and trial; with righteousness comes prosperity. Nephi shows his people their future

through Isaiah's words and strives to make them understand this lesson—
that all the coming hardship could be avoided if they would just turn to
the Lord in righteousness and follow his commandments. These first two
chapters contain a broad overview of the fate of the House of Israel.

Nephi understood that his people were a microcosm of Israel and that
they came under the same obligations as their brethren. As such, they would
follow the same fate if they took the same path. The message here should be
clear to all of us who read the Book of Mormon, for we are told that we too
are under the same obligation as the people we are reading about.

Let's take a look at Isaiah's message as found in 1 Nephi and compare
it to the Book of Isaiah by putting the two side-by-side and highlighting
the differences.

1 Nephi 20:1–2

1 **Hearken and** hear this, O house
of Jacob, **who** are called by the name
of Israel, and are come forth out of the
waters of Judah, **or out of the waters of
baptism** who swear by the name of the
Lord, and make mention of the God of
Israel, **yet they swear** not in truth nor in
righteousness.

2 **Nevertheless**, they call themselves
of the holy city, **but they do not** stay
themselves upon the God of Israel, **who is
the Lord of Hosts**; yea, the Lord of Hosts
is his name.

Isaiah 48:1–2

1 Hear **ye** this, O house of Jacob,
which are called by the name Israel, and
are come forth out of the waters of Judah,
which swear by the name of the Lord, and
make mention of the God of Israel, but
not in truth, nor in righteousness.

2 For they call themselves of the holy
city, and stay themselves upon the God of
Israel; The Lord of hosts is his name.

This is a general call to those who are the covenant people of the
Lord. Both passages make clear that he is addressing the House of Israel.[2]
However, the Nephite record contains a few differences that clarify the
passage. The first minor difference is the word *hearken* which means "pay
attention to this" and simply lends a bit more urgency to the statement.
The next difference is more significant. The biblical verse refers to the
"waters of Judah" and could simply refer to association with the House of
Israel by birth, whereas the Nephite version includes the clarifier "or out
of the waters of baptism" clearly denoting a people under the covenants
made to the House of Israel. This addition makes the next few statements

much more significant because the infractions mentioned are undertaken by people who are not just Israelites by birth, but who are also under covenant by baptism to follow the Lord! Later passages in the Book of Mormon make clear that ignorance can lead to disobedience, but sin is the knowing or willful disregard of a commandment, which is a much greater error.

The second verse contains a clarification that completely changes the tone of the biblical verse. The biblical Isaiah implies that Israel relies on the Lord. The Nephite Isaiah, however, expressly states that Israel does not rely on him. Again, the Book of Mormon adds significantly to the understanding of Isaiah while making his message more meaningful.

Armed with this insight, we are ready to scrutinize Isaiah's message, comparing as we go, that perhaps we might bring his words to life and comprehend their full meaning. In chapter 47 of the account, Isaiah had just finished pronouncing destruction and woe upon Babylon, who was the house of Judah's greatest enemy of the time, and he was now making the point that, through his prophets, the Lord had made great effort to ensure that Israel would know concerning all things to come. This was done in order to make the people see that events did not just happen randomly but that the Lord had an active hand in everything. Superstition and idol worship, very popular practices engaged in by all the surrounding civilizations of the day, were great temptations to the Israelites. Throughout the Bible, prophets had warned the Israelites not to follow after false gods and the Lord had made the prohibition of the worshipping of idols and graven images (the second and third of the Ten Commandments; see Exodus 20:1–17). Even Solomon ultimately strayed because of the false gods of his many wives.

The Israelites were always slow to acknowledge the hand of God in all their affairs and this was the cause of so much of their suffering. Nephi, likewise, had wearied of the constant battle he faced as time after time the Lord would do mighty miracles on behalf of the Nephites only to see them almost immediately forget the Lord and fall into wickedness. Nephi clearly saw that their reluctance in observing and preserving the statutes of the Lord was at the root of their problems.

Verses 3–7 of 1 Nephi 20 and Isaiah 48 make this point clear.

1 Nephi 20:3–7

3 **Behold**, I have declared the former things from the beginning; and they went forth out of my mouth, and I showed them. I did **show** them suddenly.

4 **And I did it** because I knew that thou art obstinate, and thy neck is an iron sinew, and thy brow brass;

5 And I have even from the beginning declared to thee; before it came to pass I showed **them** thee; **and I showed them for fear** lest thou shouldst say—Mine idol hath done them, and my graven image, and my molten image hath commanded them.

6 Thou hast **seen and heard** all this; and will ye not declare them? **And that** I have showed thee new things from this time, even hidden things, and thou didst not know them.

7 They are created now, and not from the beginning, even before the day when thou heardst them **they were declared unto thee**, lest thou shouldst say—Behold I knew them.

Isaiah 48:3–7

3 I have declared the former things from the beginning; and they went forth out of my mouth, and I shewed them. I did them suddenly, **and they came to pass**.

4 Because I knew that thou art obstinate, and thy neck is an iron sinew, and thy brow brass;

5 I have even from the beginning declared it to thee; before it came to pass I shewed it thee; lest thou shouldst say, Mine idol hath done them, and my graven image, and my molten image, hath commanded them.

6 Thou hast heard, see all this; and will not ye declare it? I have shewed thee new things from this time, even hidden things, and thou didst not know them.

7 They are created now, and not from the beginning; even before the day when thou heardst them not; lest thou shouldst say, Behold I knew them.

As we read this fragment it becomes apparent that the Lord is pleading with the people to acknowledge that, through his prophets, he has foretold all of the events that they have witnessed. The significance here is that while events could be ascribed to any number of causes, from simple random happenings to actions of an array of false gods or idols, none of whom could utter prophecies of the events in advance. Only a living God, that is the God of Israel, could accurately foretell the future and warn his people.

Notice that verse 3 of the Nephite record adds the word "show" to the phrase. This addition completely changes the action from one of causality to one of warning. In fact, the biblical Isaiah states the very thing the Lord is trying to dispel, that he did it without warning as opposed to the fact that he showed it before it was even suspected! The very point the Lord is making is that nothing has occurred to the Israelites (or the Nephites) without warning. Verse 5 categorically states that the Lord showed things in prophecy specifically so that the people would not be surprised. Nephi's record indicates that the Lord worried that the people might ascribe false gods or random actions to the events they were witnessing. Verse 6 of Isaiah incorrectly punctuates the first phrase making the statement sound like a commandment whereas Nephi's verse is a statement of fact, stipulating that the people have, indeed, seen and heard all things. The statement in verse 7 that "they are created now, and not from the beginning" shows that judgments are not inevitable nor are they predestined from the beginning. They are the result of unrighteous behavior of the people that suffer them. Also in this verse, we see how the addition of the declaration "they were declared unto thee" completely clears up the confusion generated by the same verse in the biblical account.

The next few verses make a very important statement to the people about the hardships and travail they are suffering. The Lord says,

1 Nephi 20:10–11

10 For, behold, I have refined thee, I have chosen thee in the furnace of affliction.

11 For mine own sake, yea, for mine own sake will I do this, **for I will not suffer my name to be polluted**, and I will not give my glory unto another.

Isaiah 48:10–11

10 Behold, I have refined thee, **but not with silver**; I have chosen thee in the furnace of affliction.

11 For mine own sake, even for mine own sake, will I do it: for how should my name be polluted? and I will not give my glory unto another.

In this instance the biblical record adds the unnecessary and possibly confusing phrase, "but not with silver."[3] The statement "I have refined thee" is strong enough to stand alone and reminds the people that the "heat" of adversity and trial can, and should, serve to make a people stronger. Just like the greater House of Israel, the Nephites had suffered many things both during their eight years in the desert and in their new home in the new land. Nephi wanted them to understand that the things they were going through could make them a strong and invincible people if they would just comprehend the greater plan.

Verse 11 contains a very interesting correction in the Book of Mormon version. Without the additional phrase "for I will not suffer my name to be polluted," we might think the Lord had an egotistical reason for working so strenuously with the house of Israel as indicated by the biblical Isaiah. However, the idea that his name might be polluted if he did not do the things he said is a reminder of the covenant that exists between the Lord and his people and that he takes his side of the covenant very seriously. The implication is that any violation on his part of the covenant would be a serious mark against his trustworthiness. It would "pollute" his name.

The next verses are a call to the people to come back to the Lord and trust in him and also to accept the words of the prophets.

1 Nephi 20:12–16

12 Hearken unto me, O Jacob, and Israel my called, for I am he; I am the first, and I am also the last.

13 Mine hand hath also laid the foundation of the earth, and my right hand hath spanned the heavens. I call unto them **and** they stand up together.

14 All ye, assemble yourselves, and hear; who among them hath declared these things **unto them**? The Lord hath loved him; yea, **and he will fulfil his word which he hath declared by them**; and he will do his pleasure on Babylon, and his arm shall come upon the Chaldeans.

15 Also, **saith the Lord; I the Lord**, yea, I have spoken; yea, I have called him **to declare**, I have brought him, and he shall make his way prosperous.

16 Come ye near unto me; I

Isaiah 48:12–16

12 Hearken unto me, O Jacob and Israel, my called; I am he; I am the first, I **also** am the last.

13 Mine hand also hath laid the foundation of the earth, and my right hand hath spanned the heavens: **when** I call unto them, they stand up together.

14 All ye, assemble yourselves, and hear; which among them hath declared these things? The Lord hath loved him: he will do his pleasure on Babylon, and his arm shall be on the Chaldeans.

15 I, even I, have spoken; yea, I have called him: I have brought him, and he shall make his way prosperous.

16 Come ye near unto me, **hear ye**

have not spoken in secret; from the beginning, from the time that it was **declared have I spoken**; and the Lord God, and his Spirit, hath sent me.

this; I have not spoken in secret from the beginning; from the time that it was, **there am I**: and now the Lord God, and his Spirit, hath sent me.

Once more we see the Lord pleading with Israel to trust him. He recounts his constancy through all time since the beginning. He clearly states that he will continue to be constant and in the long run, he will protect Israel from Babylon and Chaldea. The passage reiterates that the Lord is bound by covenant and will fulfill all his words as spoken by the mouths of his holy prophets. He also declares that the people can know all his doings before they occur if they will just listen to the prophets and give heed to their message. Certainly these verses would have been powerful words for the Nephites as Nephi struggled to establish a habit of faith in the Lord and of righteousness among his people in the new land in which they found themselves.

As this chapter ends we see the Lord urging his people to go forth in faith, knowing they will eventually be free. He reminds them that he sustained Moses and their forefathers in the desert and he also reminds them that they must live up to their side of the covenant for peace to exist among them.

1 Nephi 20:20–22

20 Go ye forth of Babylon, flee ye from the Chaldeans, with a voice of singing declare ye, tell this, utter to the end of the earth; say ye: The Lord hath redeemed his servant Jacob.

21 And they thirsted not; he led them through the deserts; he caused the waters to flow out of the rock for them; he clave the rock also and the waters gushed out.

22 **And notwithstanding he hath done all this, and greater also**, there is no peace, saith the Lord, unto the wicked.

Isaiah 49:20–22

20 Go ye forth of Babylon, flee ye from the Chaldeans, with a voice of singing declare ye, tell this, utter it **even** to the end of the earth; say ye, The Lord hath redeemed his servant Jacob.

21 And they thirsted not **when** he led them through the deserts: he caused the waters to flow out of the rock for them: he clave the rock also, and the waters gushed out.

22 There is no peace, saith the Lord, unto the wicked.

We see here an interesting thing. In verse 21 the inclusion of the word *when* in the biblical text is actually a bit clearer than in the Book of Mormon text! This should serve to remind us that both the Bible translators as well as Joseph Smith were simply working with the source materials they had. It is totally reasonable to assume that the records Nephi acquired from Laban might have had very slight differences in their transcription when compared to the records that ultimately found their way to the King James translators. That an individual word appears in one text and not in the other merely shows the individuality of the texts rather than some gross error. It is also reasonable to assume that the Joseph Smith translation, coming as it did from more original or pure documents, would have the bulk of the more pure text, but not always.

In the biblical text, verse 22 seems to pop up rather harshly and out of context. While it is a true statement by itself, what is it doing at this spot? The Book of Mormon includes the phrase, "And not withstanding he hath done all this, and greater also," which serves to tie the declaration to the fact that even though the Lord could feed and protect and quench the thirst of the people, as indicated in the previous verse, those things alone do not bring peace. This is a lesson we must learn today, for though we enjoy greater comforts and luxuries than at any time in the world before, we still seem to suffer more depression, angst, and anger than ever before. We, of all people, should be the happiest and most delightsome the world has ever known. Nevertheless, because of our wickedness, notwithstanding our wealth, comfort, and ease, we will find no peace in those things. The Lord is declaring that throughout time, the only road to peace is through righteousness.

The Manner of the Jews

As Nephi continues his recitation of Isaiah the tone of his sermon shifts from a warning and call to repentance in Isaiah 48 to a prophetic message in Isaiah 49. Here again we see the Semitic way of speaking, which always includes a balance between warning and promise. This is an easily overlooked aspect of the Book of Mormon but one that should not be ignored. At the very beginning of the Book of Mormon, Nephi states that he is making a record "which consists of the learning of the Jews" (1 Nephi 1:2). At first glance it seems insignificant that he would say such an obvious thing. However, in 2 Nephi we find a broader indication of its importance.

> Now I Nephi do speak somewhat concerning the words which I have written, which have been spoken by the mouth of Isaiah. For behold, Isaiah spake many things which were hard for many of my people to understand; **for they know not concerning the manner of prophesying among the Jews**. (2 Nephi 25:1)

To understand what he means we should take a look at our own culture. In our Western culture we tend to issue either warning or praise. Seldom do we combine the two. We say, "Don't do that or there will be a price to pay!" We make it a blanket statement and we let it stand alone. Our praise is meted out in like manner. When we do something good we hear "Good job! Here's a bonus." In fact, in our culture we are offended if we get both praise and warning. We get upset when someone says to us "You did a great job, here's a bonus—now make sure you don't foul up or there won't be any more bonuses!" We think to ourselves, "Can't he just say good job and leave it at that?"

The Middle Eastern cultures do it differently. There is always balance: the admonition and the hope, the warning and the promise. They say, "If you do not change your ways, you will suffer the consequences, but if you repent, you will be blessed." This is one of the aspects of the "learning of the Jews" that Nephi was referring to in 2 Nephi 25. He goes on in that same chapter with more explanation about this.

> Yea, my soul delighteth in the words of Isaiah, for I came out from Jerusalem, and mine eyes hath beheld the things of the Jews, and I know that the Jews do understand the things of the prophets, **and there is none other people that understand the things which were spoken unto the Jews like unto them, save it be that they were taught after the manner of the things of the Jews**. (v. 5)

Nephi continues by explaining why this would be an issue to his people:

> For I, Nephi, have not taught them many things concerning the manner of the Jews; for their works were works of darkness and their doings were doings of abomination. (v. 6)

The Nephites were not the only ones to be confused by the manner of the things of the Jews. In Acts 8 we read of an encounter between the apostle Philip and an Ethiopian eunuch who was an important member of the entourage of Candace, the Queen of Ethiopia. An angel of the Lord commanded Philip to go to the main road south of Jerusalem that led to Gaza. Along the way he encountered the Ethiopian in his chariot reading the words of Esaias[4] the prophet. We pick up the account in verse 29.

> Then the spirit said unto Philip, Go near, and join thyself to this chariot.
>
> And Philip ran thither to him, and heard him read the prophet Esaias, and said, Understandest thou what thou readest?
>
> And he said, **How can I, except some man should guide me?** And he desired Philip that he would come up and sit with him. (Acts 8: 29–30; emphasis added)

We see here that the Bible agrees with the Book of Mormon in bearing witness to the difficulty of understanding the things of the Jews. In this case it was not Nephites but an Ethiopian.[5]

It is a testimony of Joseph Smith's divine mandate to translate the golden plates that he should have included such a speech pattern in his translation.

Nephi has just read Isaiah 48 to his people to warn them and call them to repentance. He is urging them to remember the patience and longsuffering of the Lord. They have been told that it is their own disobedience that will bring upon them their hardship. It is a hard message for a proud people to hear, but it needed to be said. With that out of the way, Nephi can now balance his sermon by using Isaiah 49 to show the people the blessings that the Lord has in store for them in the last days.

1 Nephi 21:1

1 **And again: Hearken, O ye house of Israel, all ye that are broken off and are driven out because of the wickedness of the pastors of my people; yea, all ye that are broken off, that are scattered abroad, who are of my people, O house of Israel.** Listen, O isles, unto me, and hearken ye people from far; the Lord hath called me from the womb; from the bowels of my mother hath he made mention of my name.

Isaiah 49:1

1 Listen, O isles, unto me; and hearken, ye people, from far; The Lord hath called me from the womb; from the bowels of my mother hath he made mention of my name.

MARK SWINT

This addition, of what is essentially a completely new verse in the Book of Mormon account, significantly changes the tone of the call. The biblical verse could refer to people who simply live in diverse places perhaps of their own choosing. How much more appropriate is it to Nephi's people for the words to beckon a people who were "broken off," "driven out because of the wickedness of the pastors," and "scattered abroad," but who are, nevertheless "of my people, O House of Israel"? This would certainly apply to the Nephites.

In this verse Isaiah refers to his foreordination by saying he had been called from the womb. This is significant because he continues on to say, in verse 5, that his premortal call was for the purpose of bringing Jacob "again unto him" implying that the House of Israel must have been important to the Lord in the premortal life as well. This, again, would have referred back to the issue of the covenant between the Lord and the House of Israel, established in 1 Nephi 20:1.

Verses 6–10 are very prophetic but also very confusing at first reading. They almost sound as if they are talking about Isaiah the man. However, we must remember that all of Isaiah 49 is a prophecy about Jacob and the broken off portions of the House of Israel. Here is a good example of the difficulty of Isaiah's words. The key to understanding this passage is found back in verse 3.

> 3 And [the Lord] said unto me: Thou art my servant, O Israel, in whom I will be glorified.

From this we see that it is the House of Israel that is to be the Lord's servant (to the world) rather than Isaiah, who is a servant to the House of Israel. With this in mind we can now look at verses 6–10 with a much clearer understanding.

1 Nephi 21:6–10

6 And he said: It is a light thing that thou shouldst be my servant to raise up the tribes of Jacob, and to restore the preserved of Israel. I will also give thee for a light to the Gentiles, that thou mayest be my salvation unto the ends of the earth.

7 Thus saith the Lord, the Redeemer of Israel, his Holy One, to him whom man despiseth, to him

Isaiah 49:6–10

6 And he said, It is a light thing that thou shouldest be my servant to raise up the tribes of Jacob, and to restore the preserved of Israel: I will also give thee for a light to the Gentiles, that thou mayest be my salvation unto the end of the earth.

7 Thus saith the Lord, the Redeemer of Israel, and his Holy One, to him whom man despiseth, to him

whom the nations abhorreth, to servant of rulers: Kings shall see and arise, princes also shall worship, because of the Lord that is faithful.

8 Thus saith the Lord: In an acceptable time have I heard thee, **O isles of the sea**, and in a day of salvation have I helped thee; and I will preserve thee, and give thee **my servant** for a covenant of the people, to establish the earth, to cause to inherit the desolate heritages;

9 That thou mayest say to the prisoners: Go forth; to them that **sit** in darkness: Show yourselves. They shall feed in the ways, and their pastures shall be in all high places.

10 They shall not hunger nor thirst, neither shall the heat nor the sun smite them; for he that hath mercy on them shall lead them, even by the springs of water shall he guide them.

whom the nation abhorreth, to a servant of rulers, Kings shall see and arise, princes also shall worship, because of the Lord that is faithful, and the Holy One of Israel, and he shall choose thee.

8 Thus saith the Lord, In an acceptable time have I heard thee, and in a day of salvation have I helped thee: and I will preserve thee, and give thee for a covenant of the people, to establish the earth, to cause to inherit the desolate heritages;

9 That thou mayest say to the prisoners, Go forth; to them that are in darkness, Shew yourselves. They shall feed in the ways, and their pastures shall be in all high places.

10 They shall not hunger nor thirst; neither shall the heat nor sun smite them: for he that hath mercy on them shall lead them, even by the springs of water shall he guide them.

These verses are a prophecy about the Book of Mormon. The people who are called to be his servants in verse 3 will be, in verse 6, an instrument to raise up the tribes of Jacob and also will be given as a light to the Gentiles. The title page of the Book of Mormon (written in Moroni's own hand) and also the Doctrine and Covenants further reinforce and clarify this statement.

> That they may know the covenants of the Lord, that they are not cast off forever—And **also to the convincing of the Jew and Gentile** that Jesus is the Christ, the Eternal God.[6]

And also:

> Which contains a record of a fallen people, and the fulness of the gospel of Jesus Christ **to the Gentiles and to the Jews also**.[7]

Verse 8 is a bit difficult to follow, but one way to read it shows that the Lord makes the promise that they (the remnant of Israel) or at least their words, will be preserved for later generations. This is consistent with Isaiah's prophecy twenty chapters earlier that their voices would:

Speak out of the ground, and thy speech shall be low out of the dust, and thy voice shall be, as of one that hath a familiar spirit, out of the ground, and thy speech shall whisper out of the dust. (Isaiah 29:4)

Continuing in verse 8, the Lord makes reference once again to his covenant with the House of Israel. If we remember that it is through the Book of Mormon that we come to know and accept that Joseph Smith was a prophet, and that through him we come to accept the fulness of the gospel, and from the gospel we attain the blessings of the temple, then we can clearly see that the preservation of the record of these people is instrumental in bringing the covenants of the Lord back to us in this time and generation.

The prisoners mentioned in verse 9 are all of the people born since the great apostasy, who have had no access whatsoever to the fulness of the gospel. All the generations of the earth since shortly after the Savior's earthly mission have wandered in darkness not finding the gospel because it was not extant upon the earth. The coming forth of the Book of Mormon ushered in a new dispensation—the dispensation of the fulness of times—and with it a restoration of all the covenants of the Lord to his people. Because of the Book of Mormon, we have temples and the holy works performed therein, which give these same covenants to us and to our ancestors. Truly, the coming forth of the Book of Mormon is the means by which countless generations will escape the prison of ignorance and darkness, which would otherwise keep them out of the kingdom of God. It is the "light to the Gentiles" mentioned in verse 6.

Verse 10 reinforces the fact that those thus freed from prison will never again hunger nor thirst for knowledge and they will be actively led by the Savior.

As Isaiah's record continues we see an interesting inversion of chronology in his prophesy. He gives the end of the prophecy first and then gives the steps leading up to it. In verses 12–21 he foretells the eventual gathering and re-establishment of the House of Israel in the last days. He declares in verse 19 that it will be a huge event with so many people returning that,

The land of thy destruction shall even now be too narrow by reason of the inhabitants.

It is evident from verse 14 on the next page that before this gathering takes place, the people will believe they have been abandoned and forgotten. In other words, things will go badly for Israel for some time. Verses 15–16 offer the Lord's rebuttal.

1 Nephi 21:14–16	**Isaiah 49:14–16**
14 **But, behold**, Zion hath said: The Lord hath forsaken me, and my Lord hath forgotten me—**but he will show that he hath not**.	14 But Zion said, The Lord hath forsaken me, and my Lord hath forgotten me.
15 **For** can a woman forget her sucking child, that she should not have compassion on the son of her womb? Yea, they may forget, yet will I not forget thee, **O house of Israel**.	15 Can a woman forget her sucking child, that she should not have compassion on the son of her womb? yea, they may forget, yet will I not forget thee.
16 Behold, I have graven thee upon the apalms of my hands; thy walls are continually before me.	16 Behold, I have graven thee upon the palms of my hands; thy walls are continually before me.

To the reader of the biblical version the transition from verse 14 to verse 15 makes no sense. To say "The Lord hath forsaken me . . . can a woman forget her sucking child" is a non-sequitor. There is no logical flow from one thought to the other. Clearly, anyone who reads this critically would have to agree that something is missing. Here again, the beauty and value of Joseph Smith's translation is self-evident. The addition of the disclaimer "but he will show that he hath not" provides the perfect lead-in to the Lord's argument. Isaiah uses simile and metaphor to show the constancy of the Lord's attention throughout Israel's ordeal. He is saying, "What mother could forget her child? You are my children and I will not forget you."

Nephi could easily relate to this passage because of the visions he had had concerning his own people's future. As the deterioration and eventual demise of the Nephite civilization unfolded over the next thousand years, it would certainly look to the Nephites and to the outside observer that the Lord had forgotten them. In a similar manner to the Israelites, the Nephites would all be lost and only a scattered remnant of the Lamanites would remain. Continuing with the metaphor though, we see that throughout the thousand-year history of the Nephites, the Lord never failed, for even a moment, to have a prophet among the people, preaching steadfastly and prophesying continually words of warning and words of hope.

If we keep in mind that Mormon included in his abridgement only those things that are of benefit to us today, we are forced to acknowledge that, even though it feels that we as a people are spiraling downwards, we have, and have had since 1830, living prophets who are continually preaching words of warning, words of healing, and words of hope. It is amazing how appropriate Isaiah's words are both to the Nephites and to us today.

As noted earlier, Isaiah inverts his prophesy, showing the end first. Now he will show the Israelites, the Nephites, and us how the restoration is brought about. Verse 21 is the pivot point in the story. Israel still feels abandoned as she asks the Lord for an explanation:

> 21 Then shalt thou say in thine heart: Who hath begotten me these, seeing I have lost my children, and am desolate, a captive, and removing to and fro? And who hath brought up these? Behold, I was left alone; these, where have they been?

In other words, "How is it done? By what mechanism did you bring all this to pass?" This is a fair question. With the kingdom of Satan raging in the world and in the hearts of men, no one is just going to lie down and let the House of Israel re-establish itself. In fact, Satan's armies would be called to battle specifically to prevent just such an occurrence. In Satan's world nothing comes for free. Isaiah knew this, so did Nephi and all the Book of Mormon prophets. Isaiah explains, in verses 22–26 that the Lord will fight their battles and he will do it using the Gentiles.

> 22 Thus saith the Lord God: behold, I will lift up my hand to the gentiles; and set my standard to the people; and they shall bring thy sons in their arms, and thy daughters shall be carried upon their shoulders.

The word *standard,* as used here, refers to a flag. A flag represents unity of or affiliation with a group, company, army, or nation. All who are unified in a cause will "rally round the flag." The Lord is saying that he will establish his gospel and his kingdom once again upon the earth and the reestablishment of the truth will be a powerful tool to reeducate the people about the covenants of the Lord.

Continuing on we read:

> 23 And kings shall be thy nursing fathers, and their queens thy nursing mothers; they shall bow down to thee with their face towards

the earth, and lick up the dust of thy feet; and thou shalt know that I am the Lord; for they shall not be ashamed that wait for me.

24 For shall the prey be taken from the mighty, or the lawful captives delivered?

25 But thus saith the Lord, even the captives of the mighty shall be taken away, and the prey of the terrible shall be delivered; for I will contend with him that contendeth with thee, and I will save thy children.

26 And I will feed them that oppress thee with their own flesh; they shall be drunken with their own blood as with sweet wine; and all flesh shall know that I, the Lord, am thy Savior and thy Redeemer, the Mighty One of Jacob.

Nearly six hundred years later the Savior delivered the same message a little less graphically to the assembled Nephites:

These sayings which ye shall write shall be kept, and shall be manifested unto the Gentiles, that through the fulness of the Gentiles, the remnant of their seed, who shall be scattered forth upon the face of the earth . . . may be brought in, or may be brought to a knowledge of me, their Redeemer.

And then will I gather them in from the four quarters of the earth; and then will I fulfill the covenant which the Father hath made unto all the House of Israel. (3 Nephi 16:4–5)

In these passages the Lord promises to deliver us from our captors, including Satan. Satan wages war with us through ideas and temptations. Certainly, he glories when actual warfare rages, but we would be in error to think that warfare is his only tool. The greatest battles we face against Satan are personal struggles with temptation and unrighteousness. It holds, therefore, that the way we battle Satan is with righteousness and righteous living. Coming to a knowledge of the Lord and accepting his gospel is a great victory against Satan. Living that gospel steadfastly once we have accepted it will ultimately win the war.

Third Nephi 16:4 talks about the sayings that shall be written and kept, to be manifested later to the Gentiles. This is the Book of Mormon, and it is the tool the Lord will use to establish his kingdom. Through it he will bring the Gentiles to a knowledge of the fulness of the gospel. In turn, the Gentiles will bring this gospel to the House of Israel and they shall be brought to a remembrance of the covenant which the Father made with Abraham.

Over and over, we see mention of the "covenant of the Father" (Deuteronomy 4:31). This is referring to the "covenant of Abraham"

(Genesis 15:18). It is evident that the Abrahamic covenant is the template which determines the Lord's actions with respect to the House of Israel. The Book of Mormon also makes clear that all the nations and families of the earth can be blessed through this covenant and may, by accepting its precepts, be included with those who are numbered as the House of Israel.

Nephi has now concluded citing Isaiah 48 and 49, but like many of us, his people are confused and have difficulty understanding the words they have just heard. They seek clarification from him. The people's first question is, "How literal are these things?"

> What meaneth these things which ye have read? Behold, are they to be understood according to things which are spiritual, which shall come to pass according to the spirit and not the flesh? (1 Nephi 22:1)

Nephi now has the chance to speak to the people in his own words using imagery and phrasing they can understand. Having established the prophecy in the minds of the people, he can now use chapter 22, the last chapter of 1 Nephi, to make that prophecy clearer. In it he summarizes by making the following points:

- The events spoken of are literal. They will really happen.
- Because the House of Israel has fallen away, the Lord will turn to the Gentiles and make them a "mighty nation."
- He will proceed to do a marvelous work among the Gentiles.
- The Gentiles will gather the House of Israel back to the Lord.
- Through the Gentiles the house of Israel will remember the covenants of the Father and will be brought back to that covenant.
- The Gentiles who assist in this work will be numbered among the covenant people of the Lord.

This series of events that will take place in the latter days is the same story that Jacob tells during his great sermon to the Nephites in Jacob 4–6 that is known as the allegory of the wild olive branch. Interestingly, Jacob is quoting Zenos, another old world prophet whose words have been lost to the world but were obviously had among the Nephites. This is the second time we have seen Zenos quoted.

The fact that Isaiah, Zenos, Nephi, Jacob, and the Savior all dwell on the eventual gathering of Israel through the facilitation of the Gentiles shows just how fundamental to the history of the house of Israel this gathering is. It is not just a Book of Mormon story or a latter-day doctrine. It is the thread that weaves throughout all of the history of the House of Israel and all of its remnants and fragments scattered across the globe.

In Summary

Though Isaiah's words were difficult for the Nephites to understand, they were, nevertheless, a very effective tool for Nephi to use to emphasize several points. First, he urgently needed to establish and constantly remind the people that they were part of the House of Israel. Remember, the Mulekites were also of the House of Israel and yet, without records, they completely lost their identity and heritage in just a few generations. Speaking of the time that Mosiah came upon the land of Zarahemla and the Mulekites, the prophet Amaleki records the following:

> And at the time that Mosiah discovered them, they had become exceedingly numerous. Nevertheless, they had had many wars and serious contentions, and had fallen by the sword from time to time; and their language had become corrupted; and they had brought no records with them; and they denied the being of their creator; and Mosiah, nor the people of Mosiah, could understand them. (Omni 1:17)

Not only had the Mulekites forgotten the covenants of the Lord, they had also completely forgotten the Lord himself and even denied his very existence.

Nephi knew that this forgetfulness was a trait shared by all people, and he viewed his task of reminding the people of the Lord and their covenants with him as a full-time job. By citing Isaiah, whom the people recognized as a true prophet, Nephi gave his own message legitimacy in their eyes. He cleverly put himself in the position of being an expositor of another prophet's words rather than as the originator of those words. Remember, Nephi was not necessarily recognized as a prophet by all of his brethren. Thus, using Isaiah took the personal feelings of the people towards him out of the picture.

Second, Nephi needed to teach the message that is repeated throughout the Book of Mormon and taught to every generation, over and over. That is:

> Inasmuch as ye shall keep my commandments ye shall prosper in the land. (2 Nephi 1:20)

No other message was as crucial as this, for it is the fundamental message of the Book of Mormon. For over a thousand years of Nephite history we see, time and time again, that the people prospered when they were righteous and stumbled when they were not. The saddest example of this in the Book of Mormon is that, ultimately, the people's unrighteousness led to their complete and total destruction.

Mormon's whole mandate for writing his abridgement to us was to show us this principle, in as many ways as was possible. The Book of Mormon devotes 179 pages, or one-third of its content, to contention and war. The point made in all of these accounts is that enemies don't destroy a people. Rather, people are destroyed by their enemies when they become wicked. There is not a single account in the Book of Mormon where the Nephites are vanquished by the Lamanites while living righteously. The Lord used the Lamanites as an annoyance to the Nephites, to stir them up unto remembrance before the Lord when they were unrighteous, for as he said:

> And it is by the wicked that the wicked are punished. (Mormon 4:5)

Just before that statement was issued, Mormon, referring to the Nephites general state of wickedness, said;

> For were it not for that, the Lamanites could have no power over them. (Mormon 4:4)

Nephi saw and clearly understood these things and bore the task of teaching them constantly to his people. By using Isaiah, he forced the people to acknowledge his words. Nephi's use of Isaiah was brilliant and effective and, as we shall see, he returns to these words time and again.

By using the words and prophecies of Isaiah, Nephi was able to introduce certain concepts to his people without making it sound like his own words or prejudices. He had the credibility of Isaiah, a prophet recognized by even the most hardened people, to back up the words which he had just presented. By then proffering an explanation of those words to the people as he did in chapter 22, Nephi was able to accomplish his most effective teaching while people were open-minded enough to receive his words without their own prejudices. In an increasingly divided community such as Nephi's was becoming, drawing from words accepted by all was a tremendous advantage for Nephi as he struggled with the rising tide of dissension that was brewing among his people.

Notes

1. The Book of Mormon is unclear about the specific chronology of the events leading up to the death of Lehi. The best that McConkie could come up with was to say it was between 588 and 570 BC. That would be 12 to 30 years after departing Jerusalem.

2. It is correct to refer to all of Jacob's descendants as the House of Israel. However, there is also a distinction made for the split kingdoms of Israel and Judah which sometimes requires usage of the term "house of Judah" to differentiate between the northern "Kingdom of Israel" and the "Kingdom of Judah."

3. The phrase "but not with silver" makes reference to a practice that was sometimes used by dishonest goldsmiths and jewelers. In an attempt to either steal a portion of the gold they were given to work with, or to increase the weight and thereby increase the value of the piece they were making, goldsmiths were sometimes tempted to mix or "alloy" their gold with a measure of silver. This would increase the amount of metal they had to work with without changing the gold color of the metal. It was impossible to tell whether gold had been alloyed with silver without melting the object down and allowing the two metals to separate. So the much cheaper silver was sold as gold at the much higher price. Today silver is routinely alloyed with gold to make it more durable as jewelry, and this is what gives rise to the carat rating of gold. The 24-carat gold is pure while 22-, 18-, 14-carat gold has increasingly greater amounts of silver mixed in with it. The phrase as it appears in Isaiah is making the point that the Lord did his best to make the people pure and he did not hold back in any way.

4. Esaias is the Greek form of Isaiah.

5. There exist to this day a strong contingent of a people referred to as "Ethiopian Jews."

6. Title Page, Book of Mormon.

7. Ibid.

3

JACOB'S ISAIAH

Second Nephi begins at the same time, chronologically, that 1 Nephi ends. We find Nephi and Lehi before the people in what must have been much like a regular church service. Nephi spoke first and delivered a powerful sermon during which he presented some of the words of Isaiah concerning the condition of the house of Israel and likened them unto his own people. He reminded them that they were members of the house of Israel and, as such, were claimants to the blessings of the covenant of Abraham, which was extended to all the house of Israel, including those upon the islands of the sea and all the remnants scattered throughout the world. Nephi also showed them the future of the house of Israel and what things were in store for them because of their hard-heartedness and their refusal to obey the commandments of the Lord. He showed them what great blessings the Lord had in store for those who would remember the covenants and keep his commandments. Lastly, he reminded them that all could receive great blessings, even blessings of protection and prosperity if they would give heed to the Lord, obey his commandments, and live his gospel. At the conclusion of his sermon he turned the time over to his father, Lehi, to speak.

Lehi was the patriarch of all the assembled throng and he was now old and ailing. He knew his time was short, and he desired to address his posterity one last time. He took this occasion to relay to them the visions and prophesies he had continued to receive concerning them and this new land they had inherited. As he spoke, Lehi took the words Nephi had just spoken from Isaiah and likened them to his people. He pronounced prophesies concerning this new Promised Land, and he delineated the conditions upon which the people could live in peace in the land. He clearly expressed the alternative that would befall them if they forgot the statutes of the Lord, and he expressed his fear for their well-being. As we read Lehi's words we see that he was simply echoing Isaiah and putting Isaiah'a words in a contemporary setting for his posterity. After his sermon he took his younger sons, Jacob and Joseph, and gave each of them a patriarchal blessing. He then took the children of Laman, Lemuel, and Sam and blessed each of them. In each instance Lehi repeated Isaiah's message, which became the mantra of the Book of Mormon:

> Inasmuch as ye keep the commandments ye shall prosper in the land and inasmuch as ye will not keep my commandments ye shall be cutoff from my presence. (2 Nephi 4:4)

Lehi died shortly after delivering this sermon and these blessings. Sadly, his death marked the end of what little unity and peace had existed among his children and their families. It had continued to upset Laman and Lemuel, and their families and followers, that Nephi had taken the position of spiritual and political leader among the people. Approximately thirty years had passed since Lehi's family left Jerusalem and the division between the brothers and their families had become so intractable as to be irreparable. With Lehi's death, the last real bond that kept the people together broke, and they split into two groups. Nephi and those who followed him left the place where they had settled and went off into the wilderness to start anew. From this time on they became known as Nephites and it was their determination to heed and follow the warnings of all the prophets.

> And all those who were with me did take upon them to call themselves the people of Nephi.
> And we did observe to keep the judgments, and the statutes, and the commandments of the Lord in all things, according to the law of Moses.
> And the Lord was with us; and we did prosper exceedingly; for we did sow seed, and we did reap again in abundance. And we began to raise flocks, and herds, and animals of every kind.
> And I, Nephi, had also brought the records which were engraven upon the plates of brass; and also the ball, or compass, which was prepared for my father by the hand of the Lord, according to that which is written.

And it came to pass that we began to prosper exceedingly, and to multiply in the land. (2 Nephi 5:9–13)

This division of the people created a new set of circumstances for Nephi and his people. First, by removing themselves from all those who disagreed with Nephi, his support was solidified among the remainder of the people, and they firmly established him as their prophet and political leader. Indeed, Jacob says that the people did look upon Nephi "as a king or a protector, and on whom [they] depend for safety" (2 Nephi 6:2). Second, it put a schism between Nephi's people and the Lamanites, as the followers of Laman were now called, who, from this point on, became a bother and a threat to the Nephites. This perpetual threat from their brethren served to unify the Nephites and draw them around Nephi, giving him a greater voice with them.

Third, Nephi stated that he took the records that the brothers had obtained from Laban all those years ago. This meant that the Lamanites had no records among them, so it was reasonable to anticipate that within a few generations they would fall into the same condition that the Mulekites, who were living in the land of Zarahemla, were falling into. That is, they would soon forget their heritage and forget the statutes of the Lord. The Mulekites ultimately forgot the Lord and even denied his very existence. Nephi could assume that the same condition would eventually exist among the Lamanites. This would cause great sadness among the Nephites but would be a powerful and constant reminder to them of the necessity to keep the commandments of the Lord. The Lamanites would, from now on, serve as a counterpoint off which Nephi, Jacob, and the other Book of Mormon prophets could present their messages, warnings, and admonitions to their people.

Because of the split, Nephi was now free to preach more openly about the Savior and the future which lay before them, without worrying too much about those who, in the past, had openly disagreed with him. He was free to expound to a greater degree the workings and mysteries of the Lord, and we shall see evidence of this as his record progresses.

Jacob's Isaiah

After Lehi's death Nephi consecrated Jacob and gave him a holy calling to assist in the work. Jacob rose to the challenge and proved to be a strong and valiant teacher and prophet. Commencing with chapter 6 of 2 Nephi we are introduced to Jacob's words. Like his brother Nephi, Jacob had an affinity for Isaiah and started his sermon by saying that Nephi asked him to speak from the words of Isaiah.

> And now, behold, I would speak unto you concerning things which are, and which are to come; wherefore, I will read you the words of Isaiah. They are the words which my brother has desired that I should speak unto you. And I speak unto you for your sakes, that ye may learn and glorify the name of your God.
>
> And now, the words which I shall say are they which Isaiah spake concerning all the house of Israel; wherefore, they may be likened unto you, for ye are of the house of Israel. And there are many things which have been spoken by Isaiah which may be likened unto you, because ye are of the house of Israel. (2 Nephi 6:4–5)

A most curious thing happens here. Jacob quotes two verses from Isaiah 49 that were just quoted a few pages ago. They are verbatim quotes of verses 22 and 23 as found in 1 Nephi 21. This repetition, wherein something just quoted is quoted again moments later, is unique in a book of scripture. The truth is that it wasn't just moments before, though only a few pages before. Note that nearly twenty years had passed since these words were first delivered by Nephi. Since that time, a completely new generation had been born. From Jacob's declaration that Nephi wanted him to cite these words, it is obvious they had retained their importance and their applicability to his people. This passage is actually the introduction to a sermon Jacob is about to give in which he will tell them of a vision he received concerning the destruction of their ancestral home in the land of Jerusalem.

Isaiah's words are appropriate here because Jacob's own people, having landed in the new world and having established a new home (which father Lehi called their land of inheritance), were once again forced to leave when they separated from the Lamanites. Having thus become a displaced people again, they could relate to the prophesies of Isaiah concerning the scattered and fragmented house of Israel. Jacob wanted to reassure them that ultimately they would be gathered together and returned to the place of their inheritance. However, he also wanted them to know that their destiny was in their own hands. Had the Nephites been able to comprehend the connection between righteousness and prosperity, they would have avoided most of the coming adversity. Jacob explained this both with Isaiah's words as well as with his own. As he explained Isaiah to them, he said:

And after they have hardened their hearts and stiffened their necks against the Holy One of Israel, behold, the judgments of the Holy One of Israel shall come upon them. And the day cometh that they shall be smitten and afflicted.

Wherefore, after they are driven to and fro, for thus saith the angel, many shall be afflicted in the flesh, and shall not be suffered to perish, because of the prayers of the faithful; they shall be scattered, and smitten, and hated; nevertheless, the Lord will be merciful unto them, that when they shall come to the knowledge of their Redeemer, they shall be gathered together again to the lands of their inheritance.

And blessed are the Gentiles, they of whom the prophet has written; for behold, if it so be that they shall repent and fight not against Zion, and do not unite themselves to that great and abominable church, they shall be saved; for the Lord will fulfill his covenants which he hath made unto his children; and for this cause the prophet has written these things. (2 Nephi 6:10–12)

Jacob finished the chapter by referring repeatedly to Isaiah, again quoting verses from Isaiah 49. The clarity of his explanation demonstrates that he was probably as well versed in how to read Isaiah as was his older brother Nephi.

Second Nephi Isaiah Texts

In chapter 7 of 2 Nephi, Jacob again turns to Isaiah's words and begins to quote complete chapters verbatim. Thus starts the second group of Isaiah texts in the Book of Mormon.

There are actually two subgroups of Isaiah text in 2 Nephi. The first group is found in 2 Nephi 7–8. It consists of Isaiah 50 and 51 with the addition of 2 verses from Isaiah 52. It is part of a sermon delivered to the people roughly fifty years after their arrival on the American continent. The second group of Isaiah scriptures is the largest block of Isaiah found in the Book of Mormon. It covers fourteen chapters and begins with 2 Nephi 12. The text covers Isaiah 2–14. Two chapters later, 2 Nephi 27 quotes Isaiah 29.

Though the two groups appear related by their proximity in 2 Nephi, they are actually very different. The first two chapters, 2 Nephi 7–8, were in fact spoken to the Nephites in a sermon by Jacob, while chapters 12–24 were included by Nephi in his written record but were apparently not delivered by sermon to the assembled people. Chapter 27 was presented to the people as part of an extensive prophecy uttered by Nephi concerning the last days.

As Jacob begins his quotations of Isaiah we once again see some significant differences between the Book of Mormon and the biblical versions.

2 Nephi 7:1–2	Isaiah 50:1–2
1 **Yea, for** thus saith the Lord: **Have I put thee away, or have I cast thee off forever?** For thus saith the Lord: Where is the bill of your mother's divorcement? **To whom have I put thee away**, or to which of my creditors have I sold you? Yea, to whom have I sold you? Behold, for your iniquities have ye sold yourselves, and for your transgressions is your mother put away.	1 Thus saith the Lord, Where is the bill of your mother's divorcement, whom I have put away? or which of my creditors is it to whom I have sold you? Behold, for your iniquities have ye sold yourselves, and for your transgressions is your mother put away.
2 Wherefore, when I came, **there was** no man; when I called, yea, **there was** none to answer. O house of Israel, is my hand shortened at all that it cannot redeem, or have I no power to deliver? Behold, at my rebuke I dry up the sea, I make **their** rivers a wilderness and their fish to stink because the waters are dried up, and **they** die because of thirst.	2 Wherefore, when I came, was there no man? when I called, was there none to answer? Is my hand shortened at all, that it cannot redeem? or have I no power to deliver? behold, at my rebuke I dry up the sea, I make the rivers a wilderness: their fish stinketh, because there is no water, and dieth for thirst.

As with previous passages, we see how the addition of a few words can significantly alter the impact of a message. The Bible text begins this chapter with a puzzling question. In the first verse the Lord says, essentially, "I have put away your mother, where is her bill of divorcement?" As it is translated, the biblical verse makes it sound as though the Lord acted proactively, putting away the mother for reasons we know not. The balance of the verse is correctly translated but that just makes the verse more confusing. The question arises, "Who did the putting away?" In 2 Nephi the meaning of the verse is clearly stated. The Lord challenges the house of Israel with the question, "Have I put thee away?" He says, "Show me a bill of divorcement." In other words, "Where is your evidence that I have put you off? Do you have creditors holding receipts for you? No, of course not!" The Lord states clearly that it is Israel that has removed itself from him through transgression and sin, not the other way around. The biblical verse eventually says the same thing, but the confusing start renders the whole verse ambiguous and its impact is lost.

Similarly, in verse 2 of the biblical version, we find the question, "Was there none to answer?" while in the 2 Nephi version the Lord makes the declarative statement, "There was none to answer." This is a much more powerful statement and these two verses set the stage for the balance of the chapter. The Lord needs the house of Israel to understand that he has always been constant with them. He has always been there and will continue to be throughout their history. He is just as adamant, however, in reminding the people that they can distance themselves from him by sin and transgression. They can feel as though he is far away or inattentive to their needs, but it is never his doing. This is a universal lesson for all people throughout all ages. Jacob wants his people to understand that they are just as susceptible as the rest of the house of Israel to drawing away from the Lord, and he wants to remind them that the blessings of the Lord only come through diligence and faith. We can see already that these chapters of Isaiah are very appropriate for the Nephites.

In the next few verses Isaiah gives his personal testimony that the Lord will always strive with those who are humble and willing to be directed. This is in rebuttal to those who think the Lord has abandoned them.

2 Nephi 7:4	**Isaiah 50:4**
4 The Lord God hath given me the tongue of the learned, that I should know how to speak a word in season **unto thee, O house of Israel. When ye are weary** he waketh morning by morning. He waketh mine ear to hear as the learned.	4 The Lord God hath given me the tongue of the learned, that I should know how to speak a word in season to him that is weary: he wakeneth morning by morning, he wakeneth mine ear to hear as the learned.

In verse 4 we see how the change in punctuation changes the context of the message. The biblical text basically says, "That I should know how to speak to him that is weary." This could be interpreted reasonably enough to mean that Isaiah could give words of encouragement to those who had lost hope or were tired of the battle. Nephi's version, however, gives what could be seen as an even stronger promise. In his version Isaiah testifies that the Lord gives him what to say whenever it is needed, always at the appropriate time. This is the meaning of the expression "in season." The thought then continues with a new statement, "When ye are weary he waketh morning by morning," or, in other words, the Lord never tires in doing his job of warning and teaching us. Even when we tire of the battle, he never does. The 2 Nephi version of the scripture gives a richer, fuller statement about the Lord's tireless efforts on our behalf.

2 Nephi 7:7

7 For the Lord God will help me, therefore shall I not be confounded. Therefore have I set my face like a flint, and I know that I shall not be ashamed.

Isaiah 50:7

7 For the Lord God will help me; therefore shall I not be confounded: therefore have I set my face like a flint, and I know that I shall not be ashamed.

Verse 7 contains a declarative statement that Isaiah has faith and has set his face as flint, or in other words, his countenance is unflinching. He is firm in his trust in the Lord.

2 Nephi 7:8

8 **And the Lord** is near, and he justifieth me. Who will contend with me? Let us stand together. Who is mine adversary? Let him come near me, **and I will smite him with the strength of my mouth.**

Isaiah 50:8

8 He is near that justifieth me; who will contend with me? let us stand together: who is mine adversary? let him come near to me.

While the biblical verse 8 is confusing as to who is near and just who Isaiah is challenging, the Book of Mormon account shows that Isaiah feels confident that, with the Lord near, he can contend with any adversary. He testifies that the Lord will give him power to speak boldly and confound the wicked.

2 Nephi 7:9–10

9 For the Lord God will help me. **And all they who shall** condemn me, behold, all they shall wax old as a garment, and the moth shall eat them up.

Isaiah 50:9–10

9 Behold, the Lord God will help me; who is he that shall condemn me? lo, they all shall wax old as a garment; the moth shall eat them up.

10 Who is among you that feareth the Lord, that obeyeth the voice of his servant, that walketh in darkness and hath no light?

10 Who is among you that feareth the Lord, that obeyeth the voice of his servant, that walketh in darkness, and hath no light? **let him trust in the name** of the Lord, and stay upon his God.

Verse 10 poses an interesting question. Isaiah is asking, "Who among you, that do actually fear the Lord and obey his commandments, walk in darkness?" The assumed answer is no one. Everyone who trusts the Lord walks in his light. Once again we see the rare occasion in which the biblical version contains a fuller transcript of the verse than the Book of Mormon account. It adds the command, "Let him trust in the name of the Lord and stay [rely] upon his God."

As we conclude these two chapters we must consider their overall impact and determine why Jacob used them in his oration. He says,

> For I have exhorted you in all diligence; and I have taught you the words of my father; and I have spoken unto you all the things which are written, from the creation of the world. (2 Nephi 6:3)

In other words, Jacob had taught the people all things concerning their history from the beginning. In the next verse he states that he will now shift his focus to the future and read more the words of Isaiah.

> And now, behold, I would speak unto you concerning things which are, and which are to come; wherefore, I will read you the words of Isaiah. (2 Nephi 6:4)

Now Jacob talks of the present and future condition of the house of Israel. He begins by explaining that he has seen a vision of the people of Jerusalem. He has seen that they have already been carried away captive and many have been slain. His vision continues to the meridian of time and he sees the Savior's earthly mission, including his atonement and crucifixion. Jacob also sees the fate of the Jews after their rejection of the Savior, and he knows that they shall be "driven to and fro . . . they shall be scattered, and smitten, and hated" (2 Nephi 6:11), but in the latter days they shall be restored by the very Savior they rejected. He desires that the Nephites understand this series of events and that they accept the Savior as their redeemer now. Jacob uses these two chapters from Isaiah to teach his people their relationship to the Savior and his importance in their future. He wants them to understand what sad things await the people who reject his word. He does all this to the end that perhaps his own people might avoid a similar fate.

Jacob used the tenth chapter of 2 Nephi to finish his sermon to the assembled Nephites. By building on Isaiah's words, he was able to deliver a powerful discourse on the consequences of rejecting God's council and the redemption that comes through relying on Him. It is here that we find an oft-quoted verse of hope and council.

> Therefore, cheer up your hearts and remember that ye are free to act for yourselves—to choose the way of everlasting death or the way of eternal life.
>
> Wherefore, my beloved brethren, reconcile yourselves to the will of God, and not to the will of the devil and of flesh; and remember, after ye are reconciled unto God, that it is only in and through the grace of God that ye are saved. (2 Nephi 10:23–24)

After recording this excerpt of Jacob's sermon, Nephi bears witness that he, Jacob, and Isaiah have all seen the Savior and he cites the Mosaic rule that by the voice of two or three witnesses the truth of all things may be established. He says, referring to Isaiah's words,

> For I will liken his words to my people, and I will send them forth unto all my children, for he verily saw my redeemer, even as I have seen him.
>
> And my brother, Jacob, also has seen him as I have seen him; wherefore, I will send their words forth unto my children to prove unto them that my words are true. Wherefore, by the words of three, God hath said, I will establish my word. Nevertheless, God sendeth more witnesses, and he proveth all his words. (2 Nephi 11:2–3)

4

NEPHI'S ISAIAH—THE WARNING

The second body of Isaiah scriptures in 2 Nephi is the largest single excerpt found in the Book of Mormon. It is comprised of fourteen chapters, including a single block of thirteen chapters covering Isaiah 2 through Isaiah 14. At the end of that record, Nephi delivers a prophecy of his own concerning the last days and includes, in that prophecy, a recitation of the text from Isaiah 29 with some greatly embellished parts. Of all the biblical scriptures found in the Book of Mormon, this section is unique in that the first thirteen chapters were written and included in the record but not expressly spoken as a sermon to the people. Nephi explains his motivation.

> And now I write some of the words of Isaiah, that whoso of my people shall see these words may lift up their hearts and rejoice for all men. Now, these are the words and ye may liken them unto you and unto all men. (2 Nephi 11:8)

Whereas the Isaiah text just delivered by Jacob was included in Nephi's record because it contained powerful words spoken to the Nephites, these next words are additional text from Isaiah that Nephi wanted to include in his record for the benefit of future readers. In other words, these are words delivered more expressly to you and me.

While all of Nephi's account is a record kept for the purpose of educating future generations, it is generally a record of the day-to-day occurrences and developments of his people and his observations about those events. Nephi takes a break here and, like an actor making an aside on stage, he stops and talks directly to us. Though all the prophets do this on a much smaller scale throughout the Book of Mormon, this is the only time until we get to Mormon and Moroni, when we will be addressed directly by a Book of Mormon prophet and given a sermon. Nephi begins by telling us why he wants to do this.

> Behold, my soul delighteth in proving to my people the truth of the coming of Christ;
>
> And also my soul delighteth in the covenants of the Lord which he made to our fathers;
>
> And my soul delighteth in proving to my people that save Christ should come all men must perish. (2 Nephi 11:4–6)

Nephi truly loved Isaiah's words and he once again reminds all of us of their applicability to our lives. He says,

> And now I, Nephi, write more of the words of Isaiah, for my soul delighteth in his words. For I will liken his words unto my people. (2 Nephi 11:2)

We can learn the great secret to understanding the Book of Mormon if we keep constantly in our minds that everything written in its pages is a lesson to us for our times and our day. The Book of Mormon prophets are always pleading with us to learn this one great truth. When we understand this, and learn how to liken the scriptures to us, then and only then does the Book of Mormon reveal its true purpose to us. Its value as a history book is unquestionable, but its value as a guidebook for successfully navigating life in these latter days is hidden to those who do not learn this lesson.

With this perspective we can begin to examine this block of Isaiah text. A quick analysis of the chapters shows that the pattern of balancing warnings and blessings is again used. The first thirteen chapters are evenly divided with seven chapters of warning followed by six chapters of positive messages and hope.

2 Nephi 12 and Isaiah 2

This text begins with 2 Nephi 12, which is Isaiah 2. It starts out with a prophetic vision of the last days and foretells the establishment of the restored gospel "in the tops of the mountains." Verse 3 refers to the temples that will be built to administer God's ordinances (here referred to as "his ways") and mentions the two great centers of the Lord's earthly kingdom, namely Zion and Jerusalem. There is one subtle difference between the two texts in verse 2.

2 Nephi 12:2

2 And it shall come to pass in the last days, **when** the mountain of the Lord's house shall be established in the top of the mountains, and shall be exalted above the hills, and all nations shall flow unto it.

Isaiah 2:2

2 And it shall come to pass in the last days, that the mountain of the Lord's house shall be established in the top of the mountains, and shall be exalted above the hills; and all nations shall flow unto it.

The word "when" in the Nephi version doesn't seem to make as much sense as the word "that" in Isaiah. For some reason Nephi chose to begin this passage from Isaiah at chapter 2 instead of chapter 1. However, if we go back to the Bible and read Isaiah chapter 1, we find a very dark chapter about Israel's condition. Times are very bad and Israel is apostate. They have rejected the Lord's statutes at almost every turn. There is hope, however, but it will not come until the last days. In verse 25 of Isaiah 1, the Lord utters the promise that he will restore all things as at first. It is against this text that chapter 12 of 2 Nephi begins with the revelation that all these things will occur "when the mountain of the Lord's house shall be established in the tops of the mountains." In other words, verse 2 doesn't just tell us that these things will happen in the last days. It gives us an indicator of *when* in the last days they will happen. It says, "When the temples and the gospel are restored in the tops of the mountains, then will I bring to pass these things." It is a subtle difference but one that makes a strong statement. More differences become apparent as we continue reading.

2 Nephi 12:5–6

5 O house of Jacob, come ye and let us walk in the light of the Lord; yea, **come, for ye have all gone astray, every one to his wicked ways**.

6 Therefore, O Lord, thou hast forsaken thy people, the house of Jacob, because they be replenished from the east, and **hearken unto** soothsayers like the Philistines, and they please themselves in the children of strangers.

Isaiah 2:5–6

5 O house of Jacob, come ye, and let us awalk in the light of the Lord.

6 Therefore thou hast forsaken thy people the house of Jacob, because they be replenished from the east, and are soothsayers like the Philistines, and they please themselves in the children of strangers.

The Isaiah text is confusing here because it does not logically flow from "let us walk in the light of the Lord" to "therefore thou hast forsaken thy people." Anyone who reads that passage from the Bible would certainly be confused. The Book of Mormon text clarifies the essence of the verse by showing us why Isaiah beckoned the people to walk in the light of the Lord. He said, "For ye have all gone astray (and I want you to come back)." This additional scripture makes it reasonable for Isaiah to go on in the next verse and say, "Therefore, O Lord, thou hast forsaken thy people." He also says, more correctly in 2 Nephi, that the house of Jacob "hearken[s] unto soothsayers" rather than that they "are soothsayers."

The balance of chapter 12 contains quite a few small differences though the intent of the verses is generally clear. Verse 19, however, merits a closer look, for it is clarified quite a bit by the purer text.

2 Nephi 12:19

19 And they shall go into the holes of the rocks, and into the caves of the earth, for the fear of the Lord **shall come upon them** and the glory of his majesty **shall smite them**, when he ariseth to shake terribly the earth.

Isaiah 2:19

19 And they shall go into the holes of the rocks, and into the caves of the earth, for fear of the Lord, and for the glory of his majesty, when he ariseth to shake terribly the earth.

Here the additions in 2 Nephi give meaning to the phrases, "the fear of the Lord," and "the glory of his majesty," and show us why they will go into the holes and caves.

2 Nephi 13 and Isaiah 3

The next chapter of Isaiah, as found in 2 Nephi 13, is a sad tale of the consequences of sinful behavior. Again there are quite a few small differences between the Isaiah text and the Nephi text, but the message is pretty clear in both versions. The key to understanding this chapter, and probably the reason Nephi cited it, is found in verse 9.

2 Nephi 13:9

9 The show of their countenance doth witness against them, and doth declare their sin **to be even as Sodom**, and they **cannot** hide

Isaiah 3:9

9 The shew of their countenance doth witness against them; and they declare their sin as Sodom, they hide it not. Woe unto their soul! for they

it. Wo unto their souls, for they have
rewarded evil unto themselves!

have rewarded evil unto themselves.

Two important points are made with this passage. This is the first time Isaiah issues a warning for the souls of the house of Israel as opposed to just their temporal well-being. Heretofore, and in subsequent passages, Isaiah is constantly warning that things will go badly for the people as a civilization and kingdom. Here, while revealing that their sinfulness has reached Sodomic proportions, he mourns for their eternal well-being as well, saying, "Wo unto their souls." The next part of the verse repeats the very important principle Nephi wants us to understand. Isaiah says, as clearly as it can be stated, "For they have rewarded evil unto themselves." This is one of the great and primary lessons of the Book of Mormon: we determine our own fate. It is not thrust upon us by enemies or conquerors or even by wicked leaders. Isaiah is clear and Nephi obviously endorses his words when he says, "For **they** have rewarded evil unto **themselves**." This message might be obfuscated a bit because we have just read, at the beginning of this chapter, the following in verse 1:

2 Nephi 13:1

1 For behold, the Lord, the Lord of Hosts, doth take away from Jerusalem, and from Judah, the stay and the staff, the whole **staff** of bread, and the whole stay of water—

Isaiah 3:1

1 For, behold, the Lord, the Lord of hosts, doth take away from Jerusalem and from Judah the stay and the staff, the whole stay of bread, and the whole stay of water,

It sounds here as though it is the Lord who curses the people. However, we must not confuse the withholding of blessings with the pronouncement of curses. The Lord has always said he would bless Israel and provide them with food and water. The miracles of Moses in the desert in which he smote the rock and brought forth water, and the falling of Manna from heaven were the most literal examples of this. These things, however, were blessings. Withholding them from the people due to unrighteousness is a far cry from actively laying curses upon them. The Lord, because of the wickedness of the house of Jacob, withheld the blessings of food and water, leaving Israel to fend for themselves. Isaiah is very clear that it was the actions of the house of Jacob itself that rewarded evil and eternal peril unto their souls. This distinction is very important, and it is easy to see why Nephi would want his people to understand this principle.

2 Nephi 13:10–11	Isaiah 3:10–11
10 Say unto the righteous that it is well with **them**; for they shall eat the fruit of their doings. 11 Wo unto the wicked, **for they shall perish**; for the reward of their hands shall be **upon them**!	10 Say ye to the righteous, that it shall be well with him: for they shall eat the fruit of their doings. 11 Woe unto the wicked! it shall be ill with him: for the reward of his hands shall be given him.

In both these verses Isaiah lays the consequences of their actions upon their own heads. For both the righteous and the wicked he says, "They shall eat the fruit of their doings" and "the reward of their hands shall be upon them." We should remember that paganism was rampant in the days and centuries prior to Christ's birth. Even the Jews had trouble not falling into its grasp. One of the effects of paganism was that people adopted the attitude that every thing that happened to them, in the form of both adversity and blessing, came as the result of the capricious actions of offended or appeased gods. Nephi had seen, starting in the desert outside of Jerusalem, that it was far too easy for his brothers, and those who followed them, to blame either him or his father, Lehi, for all their hardships. Personal accountability and responsibility was a concept that has always eluded members of the house of Israel. These words of Isaiah were just as appropriate in Nephi's day as they were to Isaiah's audience. Since Mormon included them in his abridgement, we should assume they are just as relevant to us today.

The rest of Isaiah 3 and 2 Nephi 13 talks of the judgments that will befall a wicked people. This would be the "fruit of their doings" and "the reward of their hands" just spoken about. As this section begins it is important to point out verse 13 in both records.

13 The Lord standeth up to plead, and standeth to judge the people.

Here again we see a balance of both positive and negative in this one short verse. The message is important. Isaiah testifies that the Lord will always continue to plead but he is also willing to judge the people. This is an important verse because it talks of the doctrine found in Lehi's speech back in chapter 2 where he explained the connection between law and judgment and that without law there was neither sin nor judgment. He said in 2 Nephi 2:5, "And men are instructed sufficiently that they know good from evil. And the law is given unto men. And by the law no flesh is justified; or, by the law men are cut off."

When Isaiah said, in verse 13, that the Lord stands up to plead and stands up to judge, he was showing that before he could have grounds to judge a people, they must have been sufficiently instructed. By bearing testimony that the Lord does indeed plead with them, he is witnessing that the people about to be judged are not innocent with no knowledge of the Lord's ways, but rather people who have received his word and knowingly chosen to repudiate his counsels. This could be considered a "Fairness Doctrine" in the Lord's kingdom, and it is one that is never violated. Later in the Book of Mormon, we will see that the judgments against the Nephites were always harsher than those leveled against the Lamanites because they had received the greater light and knowledge, and thus they committed the greater sin.

The rest of this chapter is often quoted. It speaks to the daughters of Israel, but on a grander scale, it is actually speaking to the shallowness of worldliness and the fleeting nature of temporal pursuits like fame, beauty, and wealth. These verses are often heard as condemnations of worldly people outside of the Church (in almost any church for that matter), but a closer look reveals that the women the Lord refers to are "Daughters of Zion," members of the house of Israel and, more importantly, daughters who have been taught "sufficiently" to be worthy of the judgments that are about to befall them. As the two accounts are virtually identical here we will just look at 2 Nephi 13:16–24.

> 16 Moreover the Lord saith: Because the daughters of Zion are haughty, and walk forth with stretched forth necks and wanton eyes, walking and mincing as they go, and making a tinkling with their feet—
>
> 17 Therefore the Lord will smite with a scab the crowns of the head of the daughters of Zion, and the Lord will discover their secret parts.
>
> 18 In that day the Lord will take away the bravery of their tinkling ornaments, and the cauls, and the round tires like the moon;
>
> 19 The chains and the bracelets and the muffler;
>
> 20 The bonnets, and the ornaments of the legs, and of the headbands, and the tablets, and the earrings;
>
> 21 The rings and the nose jewels;
>
> 22 The changeable suite of apparel, and the mantel, and the wimples,[1] and the crisping-pins;

23 The glasses and the fine linen, and the hoods, and the veils.

24 And it shall come to pass, instead of sweet smell there shall be stink; and instead of a girdle, a rent; and instead of well set hair, baldness; and instead of a stomacher, a girding of sackcloth; burning instead of beauty.

In this whole passage, Isaiah is talking about the worldliness that comes with prosperity and being caught up in materialism. Remember though that in Isaiah's day the people were relatively poor and oppressed and it isn't clear that the women would have enjoyed such finery and fashion or demonstrated such behavior. Notice that verse 18 states, "In that day." This passage is a prophecy for future generations of Israelites who would enjoy a greater prosperity. Remember that Nephi stated in 2 Nephi 5:11, 13 that his people were enjoying a great prosperity, which was unlike anything they had experienced since leaving Jerusalem.

11 And the Lord was with us; and we did prosper exceedingly; for we did sow seed, and we did reap again in abundance. And we began to raise flocks, and herds, and animals of every kind. . . .

13 And it came to pass that we began to prosper exceedingly, and to multiply in the land.

This was a new situation for the majority of the Nephites, who had only known contention and political wrangling before separating themselves from the Lamanites. For the first time, the people were getting to see the fruits of righteousness, and it is fair for them to have enjoyed their successes. However, they were probably just like any people that suffer or are oppressed who, when they get a little prosperity, will almost immediately revel in that prosperity and sometimes forget the Lord. Nephi would have worried about this tendency among his people. He remembered the complaints of his brothers when they had had to leave their wealth and luxury back in Jerusalem to follow the Lord's commands. These words of Isaiah would have been powerful reminders to Nephi's people of the dangers they would face if they forgot the Lord. Indeed, the whole Book of Mormon is a reminder of this lesson. If Mormon truly saw our day, as he says he did, it would be perfectly understandable that this passage from Isaiah should be in our record of his people. We should always keep in mind, however, as Isaiah reminds us at the beginning of this passage, that the Lord always pleads with us before he judges us. We are always given the information and the tools we need to avoid the pitfalls of prosperity before we are blessed with it. Any people who learn this lesson can enjoy the blessings of prosperity for a long time and simultaneously find joy in living the gospel while serving the Lord.

2 Nephi 14 and Isaiah 4

After having issued such a bleak warning about the future of the house of Israel, Isaiah took one chapter to soften, for a bit, the harshness of his message by reminding the people of the blessings that ultimately awaited them in the Millennium. He would have plenty more to say concerning their wickedness later, but this little break in Isaiah 4 and 2 Nephi 14 was intended to show, unequivocally, that the Lord's way will ultimately prevail and that he will, someday, have a righteous people.

At only six verses, this chapter is short, but it portrays a lovely picture of a time when the Spirit of the Lord will reside in every home and within the heart of everyone who remains. In 2 Nephi 14:3–6 he says,

> 3 They that are left in Zion, and remain in Jerusalem, shall be called holy, every one that is written among the living in Jerusalem—
>
> 5 And the Lord shall create upon every dwelling place of Mount Zion, and upon her assemblies, a cloud and smoke by day, and the shining of a flaming fire by night: for upon all the glory of Zion shall be for a defence.
>
> 6 And there shall be a tabernacle for a shadow in the daytime from the heat, and for a place of refuge, and a covert from storm and from rain.

2 Nephi 15 and Isaiah 5

The fifth chapter of Isaiah once again utters a very dark prophecy about the nearing future of the house of Israel. As we review it, we must take note that the judgments and horror the people are about to face are brought upon them by their own actions rather than the vengeful acts of an offended God. Since 2 Nephi and Isaiah are almost identical in this chapter, we will look at just the Book of Mormon version. As the chapter begins, Isaiah stresses how diligently the Lord has striven to avert the coming tragedy. These first few verses sound very much like Zenos' "Parable of the Vineyard," which is found in the Book of Jacob, chapter 5, though they are not the same story. The book of Jacob comes right after 2 Nephi, and that parable is an account of how the Lord brings the house of Israel back from the destruction they are about to enter into here in this chapter. Second Nephi chapter 15 lays the foundation for Jacob 5.

> 1 And then will I sing to my well-beloved a song of my beloved, touching his vineyard. My well-beloved hath a vineyard in a very fruit-ful hill.
>
> 2 And he fenced it, and gathered out the stones thereof, and planted it with the choicest vine and built a tower in the midst of it, and also made a wine-press therein; and he looked that it should bring forth grapes, and it brought forth wild grapes.
>
> 3 And now, O inhabitants of Jerusalem, and men of Judah, judge, I pray you, betwixt me and my vineyard.
>
> 4 What could have been done more to my vineyard that I have not done in it? Wherefore, when I looked that it should bring forth grapes it brought forth wild grapes.

In this introduction to the chapter, the Lord is declaring that he has neither ignored nor mistreated his vineyard. He has done all that he could do, expecting a bountiful harvest, but getting instead a corrupted fruit. In keeping with Isaiah's statement that the Lord "standeth up to plead" and "standeth up to judge," this is the Lord's statement that he has pleaded sufficiently to warrant the judgments that are forthcoming.

> 5 And now go to; I will tell you what I will do to my vineyard—I will take away the hedge thereof, and it shall be eaten up; and I will break down the wall thereof, and it shall be trodden down;
>
> 6 And I will lay it waste; it shall not be pruned nor digged; but there shall come up briars and thorns; I will also command the clouds that they rain no rain upon it.
>
> 7 For the vineyard of the Lord of Hosts is the house of Israel, and the men of Judah his pleasant plant; and he looked for judgment, and behold, oppression; for righteousness, but behold, a cry.

These sad verses sound as though the Lord is wreaking destruction upon the house of Israel. However, just as we saw in Isaiah 3:10–11 (2 Nephi 13:10–11), the house of Israel has brought this destruction upon themselves. Again, the only action the Lord takes is to withhold the blessings that were keeping them safe. He does not bring destruction upon them, he merely stops keeping destruction at bay. The house of Israel was always in danger from external forces in the world. By trusting in the Lord and obeying his counsel, they earned the blessings they received from him. He had kept them safe from adversaries they could otherwise not defend against. When they forgot him and repudiated his counsels, they no longer merited the blessings that were predicated upon that obedience. This is one of the great eternal principles and we have it stated in our modern day scriptures as well. Doctrine and Covenants 130:21–22 says,

> There is a law, irrevocably decreed in heaven, before the foundations of this world, upon which all blessings are predicated.
> And when we obtain any blessing from God, it is by obedience to that law upon which it is predicated.

This eternal principle was to be both the salvation and the curse of the house of Israel. It laid the cause of their destruction solely at their own feet. All they had to do—to keep the protection of the Lord and hold their enemies at bay—was to keep the commandments upon which the Lord's blessings were predicated. Remember, one of Mormon's purposes in recording so many pages of warfare in the Book of Mormon was to show that the enemy could never prevail when the Nephites were righteous. The Nephites were vanquished only when they failed to keep the commandments. This lesson from Isaiah was fair warning to the Nephites of this principle.

The question could fairly be asked, "How did the house of Israel get into this situation?" Verses 12 and 13 in 2 Nephi 15 give us the answer.

> 12 And the harp, and the viol, and the tabret, and the pipe, and wine are in their feasts; but they regard not the work of the Lord, neither consider the operation of his hands.
> 13 Therefore, my people are gone into captivity, because they have no knowledge; and their honorable men are famished, and their multitude dried up with thirst.

Isaiah here addresses the worldliness of the house of Israel. To paraphrase a pop song, they just wanted to "party all the time, party all the time."[2] They were caught up in worldliness and riotous living and they took no time to consider the source of all their blessings. The people were not thrust into captivity but rather "gone into captivity." It was their own action and not the curse of God upon them that caused their trouble. Verse 13 says, "They have no knowledge," which should not be taken to mean that they had not heard the words of truth; rather, they had not esteemed those words as of value nor held them close. Similarly, their elders and leaders were "famished," or in other words, had not been diligent to keep themselves spiritually fed, and they were "dried up with thirst," that is, they had not quenched their thirst for righteousness with the truths of the gospel. It is clear from these passages that the house of Israel could have avoided all these troubles and gloried in the continued presence of the Lord if they had chosen to. They had received all the instruction and the tools they needed to happily thrive in the world and survive in peace and prosperity. Their lack of diligence was the source of their downfall, and they had no one to blame but themselves. Knowing, as we do, the eventual destiny of the Nephites, it is easy to see why Nephi recorded these words and why Mormon relayed them to our generation today. The forces at work upon the house of Israel are eternal principles that hold just as true today as throughout all ages of time. We are in the same jeopardy and stand eligible to claim the same blessings, as the people we are reading about.

Next in this record from Isaiah is an insight about how the House of Israel fell so far so fast. In verses 20–23 of 2 Nephi 15, we see how they had inverted the truth and perverted the value system of the day.

> 20 Wo unto them that call evil good, and good evil, that put darkness for light, and light for darkness, that put bitter for sweet, and sweet for bitter!
>
> 21 Wo to the wise in their own eyes and prudent in their own sight!
>
> 22 Wo unto the mighty to drink wine, and men of strength to mingle strong drink;
>
> 23 Who justify the wicked for reward, and take away the righteousness of the righteous from him!

These verses serve as an indictment for us today as we struggle with those who argue that abortion, homosexuality, promiscuity, and social drugs are acceptable choices while morality, virtue, respect for life, and the sanctity of marriage are considered dated and those who espouse such beliefs are intolerant. It seems apparent that it is the nature of men, when left to their own, that they will call evil good and good evil. The house of Israel did it, the Nephites did it, and we do it today. This should serve to demonstrate the applicability of Isaiah's warnings to all generations.

As this chapter of Isaiah ends, woe comes upon the house of Israel, and great and terrible judgments befall them. It sounds as though the Lord is doing these terrible things to the house of Israel because Isaiah's manner of speaking encompasses a different view. He looks upon events from an elevated view and sees how the unfolding events fit into the Lord's overall scheme of things. We tend to do the same thing today. We see world events unfold as people go about the business of living. They suffer the consequences of their wise and unwise decisions. As wars and various intrigues occur, we can easily attribute them to the actions of unwise men, yet from a broader perspective, we can judge them against the template of heavenly edict. We say to ourselves, "What do you expect when men live so wickedly?" We innately understand that sadness follows unrighteousness, but we don't blame God for that sadness. Verse 24 of Isaiah 5 pronounces frightful judgments upon the people; however, Isaiah is quick to explain why the judgments befall them.

> Therefore, as the fire devoureth the stubble, and the flame consumeth the chaff, their root shall be rottenness, and their blossoms shall go up as dust;

The first half of the verse pronounces the destruction of the people because they have become like chaff and stubble. The second half of the verse tells why this is so.

> Because they have cast away the law of the Lord of Hosts, and despised the word of the Holy One of Israel.

Their destruction was brought about because they ignored the law and refused to hear the words of the Lord and his prophets. Isaiah said they became as stubble and chaff.

After the harvest, when the fruit has all been gathered, the stubble and the chaff are all that is left. There is no nutritional value in them, so they are burned to clear off the field for the next season's crop. In like manner, the house of Israel had become stubble, with no good fruits coming forth from among them. They needed to be cleared away so the Lord could raise up a fresh new crop of fruitful people. And yet, it was not the Lord who would "burn the field." Rather it was the people themselves who, through unrighteous living, would bring about their own destruction. Mormon said, "And it is by the wicked that the wicked are punished." We are once again reminded of the recurring example in the Book of Mormon in which the Nephites were never conquered by the Lamanites when they lived righteously.

2 Nephi 16 and Isaiah 6

Second Nephi 16 and Isaiah 6 start with Isaiah's own personal redemption and his calling as a prophet. In it he states that he volunteered to be the one to take this message of the Savior to the house of Israel. The Book of Mormon account clarifies verse 9 so that the rest of the chapter makes sense.

2 Nephi 16:9	**Isaiah 6:9**
9 And he said: Go and tell this people—Hear ye indeed, but **they understood** not; and see ye indeed, but **they perceived** not.	9 And he said, Go, and tell this people, Hear ye indeed, but understand not; and see ye indeed, but perceive not.

Nephi's record shows that it was the people who refused to hear and see instead of the confusing implication of the biblical Isaiah, which makes it sound as though the Lord was intentionally blocking the people's understanding. The clarification in Nephi makes verse 10 easier to understand.

> 10 Make the heart of this people fat, and their ears heavy, and shut their eyes—lest they see with their eyes, and hear with their ears, and be converted and be healed.

This verse seems tinged with sarcasm, which in this case might be acceptable, since the solution to all of the problems faced by the house of Israel could easily be solved if they would just listen to their prophet and heed his words. Obviously, Nephi could relate to Isaiah's frustration, and he surely wanted his people to avoid becoming stubble and chaff like the greater house of Israel.

The last three verses of the chapter contain a prophecy that refers to Nephi's people directly while at the same time foretelling the complete destruction of the house of Israel in the holy lands.

> 11 Then said I: Lord how long? And he said: Until the cities be wasted without inhabitant, and the houses without man, and the land be utterly desolate;
>
> 12 And the Lord have removed men far away, for there shall be a great forsaking in the midst of the land.
>
> 13 But there shall be a tenth, and they shall return, and shall be

eaten, as a teil-tree,[3] and as an oak whose substance is in them when they cast their leaves; so the holy seed shall be the substance thereof.

Verse 12 speaks of the men removed far away because of the great forsaking in the land. Recall that the Lord's instruction to Lehi was to remove his family from Jerusalem because a great destruction was coming to the land.[4] This utterance by Isaiah was spoken one hundred years prior to that time, but it accurately foresaw the destruction of Jerusalem and the establishment of Lehi's family in the new world. No wonder then that Nephi would record these words for his own people and their descendants.

Verse 13 holds out the promise that someday the house of Israel will be restored and the remnant of these people who have been removed will return. More important, the holy seed, or the gospel shall be with them. It is not an unreasonable interpretation to view the Book of Mormon as that "holy seed" that is the "substance thereof."

2 Nephi 17 and Isaiah 7

After five consecutive chapters of warning and foreboding, we are finally at Isaiah 7, which is a unique and difficult chapter to interpret, but one that contains a clear and direct prophecy about the Savior. Unlike the previous chapters where, under careful and close reading, they grudgingly surrender their meaning to us, chapter 7 is impossible to understand without a knowledge of late eighth century BC Judean history. The chapter is addressed to Ahaz, the king of Judah, who ruled from about 740 BC to about 724 BC.[5]

Ahaz was the grandson of King Uzziah and the son of King Jotham, two kings who had built Judah up to be a sovereign nation. Unlike his predecessors, Ahaz was a wicked and an idolatrous man, choosing to worship the false god Molech rather than the God of his own people, Jehovah. Ahaz had even sacrificed his own two sons in a ritual to Molech in which they were burned alive.

Though the Lord still supported Judah, he was wroth with Ahaz and so withdrew his protection for Judah as a country. During the sixteen-year reign of Ahaz, Judah lost its freedom and became a vassal of Assyria. The Lord was still with the people of Judah though, and he brought about miracles on their behalf.

On one occasion, prior to the times referred to in Isaiah 7, the armies of Ephraim[6] invaded the kingdom of Judah and kidnapped 200,000 wives and children of their warriors for the purpose of putting them into slavery. The Lord sent a prophet to confront the conquering army and express his anger toward them for the deed. The invaders were humbled, and they returned the captives to Judah, even providing food and medicine for their restoration. Even with such a magnanimous act from a loving God, Ahaz still could not humble himself sufficiently to put his personal faith in the Lord, and so the destruction of his kingdom proceeded. Later the combined armies of Israel and Syria came upon Judah again, and the Lord sent another prophet to Ahaz with a message and an offer of help, but once more Ahaz refused to trust the Lord. This time it was Isaiah who was sent and it is this event that is recorded in Isaiah 7.

This is all very obscure history to us today and even with the details of these events, we cannot fully put this chapter into perspective. However, it was recent history to Nephi's people and was undoubtedly taught to the Nephites as part of their secular education. Nephi was certainly aware of the story of Ahaz before citing Isaiah in his record. When we come to realize—as the story of Ahaz demonstrates yet again—that the Lord will not totally forsake his people, we can begin to understand how Nephi was drawing a parallel to Ahaz's time with the times he saw coming, during which his own people would be under less righteous rule. When Nephi was recording these words, his people were righteous, but he had seen in vision the times ahead and knew that it would not always be so. Perhaps that is the reason this passage was more appropriate for his unspoken record rather than for a live sermon.

The verbiage in Isaiah 7 and 2 Nephi 17 are virtually identical and they speak to the threat of Ephraim and Syria, in combination, coming up against Judah. The Lord issues a call to Isaiah to go to Ahaz with an offer of help that will require that Ahaz repent and have faith in the Lord. Isaiah delivers the Lord's message, which is that the two nations will come upon Judah and, if Ahaz does not repent, Judah will not survive intact.

> 9 And the head of Ephraim is Samaria, and the head of Samaria is Remaliah's son. If ye will not believe, surely ye shall not be established.

History shows that, indeed, Ahaz did not believe in God, thinking that he stood a better chance by aligning himself with the king of Assyria to whom he was forced to pay a hefty tribute. The union worked and the invading tribes from the north were driven back, but the cost of the victory was severe for Judah. Ahaz was forced to plunder the gold and treasure of the temple to pay the king, and Judah became a vassal state of Assyria.

During his visit with Ahaz, Isaiah offered the king a chance to seek a sign from the Lord, as a test of his true mission, but Ahaz would not hear of it. In frustration, Isaiah went ahead and uttered a messianic prophecy from the Lord, which was as direct as any seen thus far in the record.

> 14 Therefore the Lord himself shall give you a sign; Behold, a virgin shall conceive, and bear a son, and shall call his name Immanuel.
>
> 15 Butter and honey shall he eat, that he may know to refuse the evil, and choose the good.
>
> 16 For before the child shall know to refuse the evil, and choose the good, the land that thou abhorrest shall be forsaken of both her kings.

The Lord was trying to give hope to Israel by confirming that the Messiah would yet come. This implied that Ephraim and Syria would themselves be vanquished,[7] and Israel would be freed from their oppression. The message was that Ahaz should be patient and humble and have faith in him. Knowing that he would not, the Lord continues with a prophecy about the consequences of his alliance with Assyria.[8]

> 17 The Lord shall bring upon thee, and upon thy people, and upon thy father's house, days that have not come from the day that Ephraim departed from Judah, the king of Assyria.
>
> 18 And it shall come to pass in that day that the Lord shall hiss for the fly that is in the uttermost part of Egypt, and for the bee that is in the land of Assyria.
>
> 19 And they shall come, and shall rest all of them in the desolate valleys, and in the holes of the rocks, and upon all thorns, and upon all bushes.

As we know from the origins of the Book of Mormon, it was just over one hundred years later that Nebuchadnezzar came down and took Judah captive back to Babylonia. Palestine and Judea were left desolate to the house of Judah, and when Judah did return to Jerusalem, they did so under the rule of others for the rest of their time in the Holy Land. In fact, there was never again an independent Israel until 1947.

Having so clearly prophesied about the birth and advent of the Savior, even as he was pronouncing such great woe upon Judah, Isaiah now used the following chapter to change his emphasis and concentrate on the Messianic prophecies and the dark, near future of the house of Israel. He begins by contrasting the relative virtues of putting your trust in worldly strength versus putting that trust in God. In this manner Isaiah 8 sounds like a negative chapter, but really the Lord is just presenting the two different courses available to the house of Judah. He uses this chapter to clearly show, through prophecy, the consequences of both actions. We are in a portion of Isaiah in which the records of Isaiah and 2 Nephi are almost word for word identical,[9] so we will just cite 2 Nephi.

2 Nephi 18 and Isaiah 8

Second Nephi 18 and Isaiah 8 begin with reference to Maher-shalal-hash-baz and to a prophetess. According to Bible historians this was Isaiah's son and the prophetess referred to was his wife. The name Maher-shalal-hash-baz means "plunder speedeth, spoil hasteth"[10] or in other words, plunder and spoil are coming quickly to the land. In this case the land is the land of Assyria. Verse 4 states that the boy will not even be old enough to speak to his parents before these things shall come to pass. The point the Lord wanted to make to the house of Judah here was that they were wrong to assume that by allying themselves to the King of Assyria they would enjoy the riches and prosperity of his kingdom. This would prove true on two counts. First, the alliance with Assyria would cost King Ahaz and the house of Judah dearly because of the tribute required for Assyria's protection. Second, Assyria would not stand long before they would see their own riches disappear.

This political alliance is very possibly the foundation for scriptural prohibitions to "neither trust in the arm of flesh" (2 Nephi 4:34; D&C 1:19; 2 Chronicles 32:8). Their failure to learn this lesson and heed this warning from Isaiah cost the house of Judah their freedom and marked the end of a true independent kingdom for them. From this point on they were the property of the Assyrians, the Maccabees, the Greeks, and the Romans before finally being driven from their land of promise once and for all. Verses 6–8 show the offer the Lord held out to them and the consequence of choosing instead to trust in men.

> 6 Forasmuch as this people refuseth the waters of Shiloah that go softly, and rejoice in Rezin and Remaliah's son;
> 7 Now therefore, behold, the Lord bringeth up upon them the waters of the river, strong and many, even the king of Assyria and his glory; and

he shall come up over all his channels, and go over all his banks.

8 And he shall pass through Judah; he shall overflow and go over, he shall reach even to the neck; and the stretching out of his wings shall fill the breadth of thy land, O Immanuel.

The reference in verse 6 to the "waters of Shiloah" is interesting in that it has two different but equally appropriate interpretations. Shiloah was in fact a sacred city about ten miles north of Palestine where the tabernacle and the Ark of the Covenants resided until the battle of Ebenezer took them away. "The waters of Shiloah that go softly" could have referred to the peace that reigned in Shiloah during its glory days. However, since Isaiah was speaking messianically here, we might also consider the less obvious but equally true fact that the word *Shiloah,* as confirmed by the Joseph Smith translation of the Bible, is a prophecy about the Messiah (JST, Genesis 50:24) and the fact that he would indeed be of the actual royal lineage of David and as such be an heir to the throne. *Shiloah* can be translated as "he to whom it belongs" (Ezekial 21:27). So the Lord was saying to the house of Judah: "Since you refuse to be under the kingship of the Messiah and choose instead to be under the kingship of Rezin, this is what will happen to you." Verses 7 and 8 describe how the kingdom of Assyria will literally overrun the kingdom of Judah. The imagery used is of the Tigris River (site of Nineveh, capitol of Assyria) overflowing its banks.

Verses 9 and 10 reiterate the warning about the consequences of trusting in the arm of flesh.

9 Associate yourselves, O ye people, and ye shall be broken in pieces; and give ear all ye of far countries; and gird yourselves, and ye shall be broken in pieces; gird yourselves and ye shall be broken in pieces.

10 Take counsel together, and it shall come to naught; speak the word, and it shall not stand; for God is with us.

It is interesting that verse 9 repeats the "gird yourselves" phrase as if to make it more certain. Verse 10 is confusing because it sounds like God's association with them doesn't do any good. After all, their plans will still fail and their words will not stand. Perhaps the verse would be easier to understand if we pretended that the sentence continued on by saying, "For God is with us in spite of ourselves and in spite of our plans and counsels." In the end, He will let neither Judah nor the larger house of Israel fall. This is actually what Isaiah was intending to say. He wanted the house of Judah to understand that in the long term their fate was directed by God and not them. The Lord would allow this generation to put themselves into bondage, and because of their actions their children and their children's children, would suffer, but the house of Judah, in the long view, was under the guidance of God and there were still things he needed to accomplish with it.

The Lord then gives Isaiah personal instruction to eschew the ways of Judah and Israel. He specifically tells him not to seek or endorse any alliance with any outside or foreign power for protection.

> 11 For the Lord spake thus to me with a strong hand, and instructed me that I should not walk in the ways of the people, saying:
> 12 Say ye not, A confederacy, to all to whom this people shall say, A confederacy; neither fear ye their fear, nor be afraid.

Verse 13 is also specifically for Isaiah, telling him where his strength and his security should be found.

> 13 Sanctify the Lord of Hosts himself, and let him be your fear, and let him be your dread.

Verse 14 is another of those confusing verses where the meaning is obscured by its syntax.

> 14 And he shall be for a sanctuary; but for a stone of stumbling, and for a rock of offense to both the houses of Israel, for a gin[11] and a snare to the inhabitants of Jerusalem.

Here again we can better understand what the Lord was telling Isaiah if we break the verse apart and throw in a clarifier. The phrase "And he shall be for a sanctuary" was directed to Isaiah alone, referencing the preceding verse. The rest of the verse becomes clearer if we modify the statement as follows: "*But, for the houses of Israel, he shall be* a stone of stumbling." The prophecy continues in verse 15, which further clarifies what is about to befall the house of Judah.

> 15 And many among them shall stumble and fall, and be broken, and be snared, and be taken.

The question should be asked here, "How is the Lord the stumbling block and why is he the one doing the trapping and snaring?" The truth is that the Lord isn't their enemy, and he is not the one doing the trapping. He had offered to be their sanctuary just like he would be for Isaiah. The house of Judah had the law and the teachings of the prophets. But because they had the light of truth, their actions were not just errors of bad judgment or ignorance. Rather, they were violations of the law they knew. They were committing sin against the light, and it is sin that brings people into the bondage of the devil. Isaiah's manner of speaking may be confusing, but his message is pure doctrine. He says here, "Because you have received the law, you are bound to a higher standard and obligation to that law. When you repudiate it, you sin against the greater light and you stumble and fall farther than had you not ever received it in the first place."

This reality, that to whom much is given much is expected, is to be a recurring theme throughout the Book of Mormon history. On many occasions the Nephites were only guilty of doing the same things that the Lamanites were doing. For the Lamanites those actions were transgressions of the natural order of things, and so they suffered the consequences of that disruption. The Nephites, however, were guilty of violating not only the "right way" of doing things but also of going against clearly spelled-out statutes that had proscribed such actions. Their offense was greater and because of that they were in sin, which brings its own consequences above and beyond the natural consequence that life metes out. Nephi wanted his people to understand that the law is an obstacle on the pathway to sin and it becomes a stumbling block to all who would try to get around it. Isaiah's words were very appropriate for the Nephites and they are very appropriate for us today.

As chapter 18 concludes, Isaiah testifies that he and his disciples will rely on the Lord and the Law.

> 16 Bind up the testimony, seal the law among my disciples.
>
> 17 And I will wait upon the Lord, that hideth his face from the house of Jacob, and I will look for him.
>
> 18 Behold, I and the children the Lord hath given me are for signs and for wonders in Israel from the Lord of Hosts, which dwelleth in Mount Zion.

It seems to be a law of civilization that wherever wickedness rages upon the face of the earth, there will always be a handful of truly righteous people that will continue in the ways of the Lord. Perhaps Sodom is the only example where the Lord challenged Lot to find just ten good men among the people and he could not (Genesis 18:26–32). And yet, even there, Lot and his family were spared to wait upon and serve the

Lord. Once more we see a common thread between Isaiah and his family and the history and circumstances of Lehi's family. Isaiah was called not only to preach the word but also to preserve that word while the rest of the people refused it. He tells what will befall them as they wander without the light of the gospel active in them.

> 19 And when they shall say unto you, Seek unto them that hath familiar spirits, and unto wizards that peep and mutter—should not a people seek unto their God for the living to hear from the dead?
>
> 20 To the law and to the testimony; and if they speak not according to this word, it is because there is no light in them.
>
> 21 And they shall pass through it hardly bestead[12] and hungry; and it shall come to pass that when they shall be hungry, they shall fret themselves, and curse their king and their God, and look upward.
>
> 22 And they shall look unto the earth and behold trouble, and darkness, dimness of anguish, and shall be driven to darkness.

From these last few verses, we see that the body of the house of Judah in particular, and the house of Israel in general, will continue to spiral downward into ever increasing darkness and ever further away from the light until finally, their kingdom is gone and their glory has vanished. As Nephi wrote these words in his personal records, it is sad to remember that he had most certainly seen the destruction of his own people one thousand years hence and, being so familiar with Isaiah, he found a familiar voice in his words of warning. This chapter would foretell the end of what little glory remained in Israel. There could be no more to say. Now it would be time to speak of the future and of an ultimately happier state of Israel in the last days.

Notes

1. A wimple was a cloth covering worn about the head and chin by late medieval women, especially nuns.
2. Eddie Murphy, "Party all the Time" written by Rick James. Sony records, 1985.
3. Teil tree is an old name for the Lime tree, also known as Terebinth or "Turpentine tree." Smith's Bible Dictionary.
4. See 1 Nephi 1:13 and 1 Nephi 2:2
5. Biblical scholars are uncertain of the chronology of Judah during this

epoch. All dates are approximations.

6. All of northern Israel was called by the name of Ephraim, the most dominant tribe.

7. According to 2 Nephi 17:8, this happened "threescore and five" or sixty-five years from then.

8. Syria and Assyria (which means "above Syria") are not to be confused as they are vastly different. Syria was originally known as Aram and is to this day the land north of Palestine. In those days, its territory stretched a bit farther west of Palestine as well. Its people are Semites and were descended from the same stock as the Israelites, though they were generally rivals. In the third century BC, Syria actually ruled over Palestine.

   The Assyrians were mostly of Semitic origin and spoke a Semitic language. However, they seemed to have a great deal of cultural influence from some earlier civilization. They later became part of the Babylonian empire. Living along the Tigris River in what is today northwest Iraq, they held Nineveh as their capital. Mosul, across the river, and Babylon were long their rivals. During the late seventh century BC, Assyria fell under the Medes (Persians) while Syria came under control of Babylonia.

9. We have seen, in this most recent group of Isaiah texts that the two transcripts are much more aligned than the earlier passages we have read. Biblical scholars have long surmised that the book of Isaiah was written by as many as three different authors due to the subtle differences in style and composition. However, the fact that Nephi had the record of Isaiah a mere one hundred years after its initial writing would seem to suggest that the record is indeed attributable to the stated author. The fact that these first chapters of Isaiah are much closer to the 2 Nephi texts on a word for word basis suggest that the King James translators were perhaps working with source materials that had been compiled from multiple transcribers at some earlier date. We must remember that we do not have a single biblical transcript that dates from about AD 900. It is very likely that earlier translators and transcribers could have engaged in collaborative efforts to finish the work and individual styles may have had occasion to slip into the record.

10. ChristianAnswer.net

11. Or trap. Used for hunting small animals, it is usually a noose made from wire or cord.

12. Hard pressed, greatly distressed. This is the only time this word is used in the King James Bible. It is a translation of the Hebrew word *Qashah*, meaning "to oppress or be in times of hardship; to be stubborn." Strong's Concordance of the Bible.

5

NEPHI'S ISAIAH—THE HOPE

The second half of Nephi's Isaiah text provides the hopeful balance for the first seven chapters that's just concluded. The story of the house of Israel and the house of Judah is not dissimilar to the story of the Nephites and the Lamanites. Just as the Israelites were displaced from their home in Egypt and made to wander in the desert for many years, so too, the family of Lehi was compelled to leave the land of Jerusalem (which was under the control of the Egyptian Pharaoh, Necco II) and likewise wander in the desert for many years. Once established in their promised land, the Israelites only made it through three kings before divisions among the people caused the kingdom to split and become the kingdoms of Israel and of Judah. Lehi's people stayed together for far less time than the Israelites before dividing into the Nephites and the Lamanites.

For the kingdoms of Israel and Judah, one history would have been lost completely to the world while the other would be driven, smitten, and diminished. In like manner, the house of Lehi would see the Nephite people completely lost while the Lamanites would be driven, smitten and diminished. The Lord promised the house of Israel that they would one day be gathered together again and be restored to fulfill their divinely mandated mission. So too, the Nephite record, speaking from the dust, would one day be the cause of a great restoration to the Lamanites and would lead to the restoration and bringing forth of the fulness of the gospel to all the families on the earth. In almost every way, the story of the house of Lehi is an allegory of the history of the whole house of Israel.

This similitude is not by chance nor is it coincidental. As the family of Jacob became the house of Israel, it was the youngest brother, Joseph, who was separated from the rest of his family, eventually ending up in the foreign land of Egypt. There he established himself and gained great power with the Pharaoh. Foresight and divine guidance caused him to store the provisions and food that would eventually be the source of salvation during a famine, not only for the Egyptians but for his own family as well. He would be the cause of their gathering in this foreign land, and he would save them.

As descendants of Joseph, Lehi's family would leave the rest of their people and travel to a foreign land. There they would establish themselves and prosper for a time. But the good times would not last and their prophets would see the coming spiritual famine. They would store—in the form of records, prophecies, and visions—the spiritual food necessary to save their people when the famine hit. Today, the Book of Mormon is to us what all the food in the storehouses of Egypt was to the Egyptians as well as to Israel and his family. It provides the spiritual food to nourish the famished nations of the earth, and the value it brings to the world will be the cause of the restoration and salvation of the house of Israel in the last days.

Nephi knew and understood well that any words spoken by Isaiah, as one of the last great prophets of Judah, could be applied to any of the scattered fragments of the greater house of Israel. He knew that the words of Isaiah were spoken as directly to his own people as they were to Judah in Isaiah's day. In fact, Nephi's people were probably among the first to truly consider them, as Isaiah speaks of his own people's reluctance to see or hear anything from God.

The previous seven chapters of Isaiah and 2 Nephi have spelled out a pretty gloomy scenario for all the Israelites, in spite of the fact that the Lord and Isaiah continually showed them how to avoid the coming peril and doom. In the next six chapters Isaiah takes the time to show the house of Israel what great things the Lord has in store for them in the last days. These are blessings that could have been had by the early Israelites but, sadly, it appears that only those in the last days will be humble enough to read, consider, and ponder them and then take advantage of them.

Isaiah has issued dire warnings to the house of Israel and now it is time to present a message of hope. This is not meant to obviate the warning but rather to balance it and show the people that they are free to choose their own fate. Both paths are out there, and it is up to the individual to choose which way he will go, as Jacob says:

Therefore, cheer up your hearts, and remember, ye are free to choose for yourselves—to choose the way of everlasting death or the way of eternal life. (2 Nephi 10:23)

2 Nephi 19 and Isaiah 9

This second part begins with 2 Nephi 19 and Isaiah 9. Isaiah once again speaks about the Messiah. He shows that the hope of Israel lies in the Savior, who is yet to be born. The Savior is first referred to as a great light.

> 2 The people that walked in darkness have seen a great light; they that dwell in the land of the shadow of death, upon them hath the light shined.
>
> 3 Thou hast multiplied the nation, and increased the joy—they that joy before thee according to the harvest, and as men rejoice when they divide the spoil.
>
> 4 For thou hast broken the yoke of his burden, and the staff of his shoulder, the rod of his oppressor.

The "land of the shadow of death" mentioned in verse 2 is a direct reference to David's 23rd psalm wherein he says, "Yea, though I walk through the valley of the shadow of death" (Psalm 23:4). It refers to the world and says that the light has come forth in the midst of darkness. The statements and promises of verses 3 and 4 indicate that Isaiah is talking about the second coming of the Savior rather than the time of his mortal ministry, though his birth certainly brought great light into the world.

It is after this passage that we encounter one of Isaiah's well-known statements, from which Handel took inspiration for his famous work "The Messiah."

> 6 For unto us a child is born, unto us a son is given; and the government shall be upon his shoulder; and his name shall be called Wonderful, Counselor, The Mighty God, The Everlasting Father, The Prince of Peace.
>
> 7 Of the increase of government and peace there is no end, upon the throne of David, and upon his kingdom to order it, and to establish it with judgment and justice from henceforth, even forever. The zeal of the Lord of hosts will perform this.

After these famous verses, Isaiah's text becomes more confusing. He makes it sound, at first reading, as if the Lord is pronouncing more curses upon Israel. However, what Isaiah is really talking about is the purification of the Israelites and the house of Judah. Isaiah refers to Assyria, saying that they, along with the Philistines, will be one of the means by which Judah shall be cleansed. He says they shall "devour Israel with open mouth" (2 Nephi 19:12). This need to cleanse Israel is because "every one of them is a hypocrite and an evildoer, and every mouth speaketh folly" (2 Nephi 19:17). Isaiah says, speaking of Judah, that the Lord will cut off the head and the tail, the branch and the rush from Israel and will do it swiftly.

14 Therefore will the Lord cut off from Israel head and tail, branch and rush in one day.

15 And the ancient, he that is the head; and the prophet that teacheth lies, he is the tail.

16 For the leaders of this people cause them to err; and they that are led of them are destroyed.

One of Isaiah's primary complaints with the house of Judah was with its leadership. He was constantly railing against those who would lead the people into paths of wickedness.

The leaders were the ones who interpreted and administered the law and they had enormous power to affect the public behavior and perceptions about everything from social order to proper worship of the Lord. Isaiah obviously believed that the people were being led astray by their leaders and he declared loudly and clearly that the Lord would not stand for it in the end.

If, in fact, the "Prince of Peace" were going to come to the house of Judah, the people would need to be in a condition to receive him. They would need to be of a mindset whereby they could follow him and perceive his rule and his guidance to be of value to them. The Lord would not be able to be the king of a people who repudiated his teachings and counsel. Therefore, this chapter and the one that follows were given to alert the people that the Lord would do all that was necessary to cleanse the house of Judah before the Prince of Peace began his reign.

2 Nephi 20 and Isaiah 10

Isaiah 10 and 2 Nephi 20 continue this theme with Isaiah stating the nature of Israel's sins. He says:

1 Wo unto them that decree unrighteous decrees, and that write grievousness which they have prescribed;

2 To turn away the needy from judgment, and to take away the

right from the poor of my people, that widows may be their prey, and that they may rob the fatherless!

The Lord is no happier with Assyria than he is with the house of Judah, but he gives them the charge to be the source of scourging and cleansing for Judah. Remember, Mormon said that it is by the wicked that the wicked are punished (Mormon 4:5). Here is a perfect example of that principle. In verse 6 the Lord says:

> 6 I will send him against a hypocritical nation, and against the people of my wrath will I give him a charge to take the spoil, and to take the prey, and to tread them down like the mire of the streets.

He is referring here to the king of Assyria. Isaiah takes a few verses to explain that the king of Assyria will think he is being victorious and doing these things himself through his considerable power. However, it is the Lord who is allowing the king of Assyria to come upon the house of Judah.

Isaiah speaks the mind of the Assyrian king in the next few verses. We should not confuse his voice with that of the Lord. In verse 10, "As my hand hath founded the kingdoms of the idols" is referring to the hand of the king of Assyria, not the hand of the Lord. In fact, in verse 12 the Lord says that once the cleansing work is complete he will punish the "stout heart" of the king of Assyria and vanquish his pride.

Isaiah pretends to speak for the king once more in verses 13–14, demonstrating his egotistical and prideful manner.

In verse 15, Isaiah clearly shows that the king of Assyria was merely a tool in the hands of the Lord to bring about his higher and nobler purposes and that his confidence in his own strength is misplaced.

> 15 Shall the ax boast itself against him that heweth therewith? Shall the saw magnifieth itself against him that shaketh it? As if the rod should shake itself against them that lift it up or as if the staff should lift up itself as if it were no wood!

Finally, Isaiah declares, the Lord will come, and when he does, those of the house of Israel who remain shall turn to him. The apocalyptic event shall be the final day of cleansing, and the wicked shall be consumed as stubble in the field.

> 17 And the light of Israel shall be for a fire, and his Holy One for

a flame, and shall burn and shall devour his thorns and his briers in one day;

23 For the Lord shall make a consumption, even determined in all the land.

Then the Lord offers hope for the remnant of Jacob, those of all the tribes of Israel who have become pure and strong in the Lord. He encourages them saying,

24 Therefore, thus saith the Lord God of Hosts: O my people that dwellest in Zion, be not afraid of the Assyrian; he shall smite thee with a rod, and shall lift up his staff against thee, after the manner of Egypt.

25 For yet a little while, and [then] my indignation shall cease, and mine anger [shall turn] in their destruction.

26 And the Lord of Hosts shall stir up a scourge for him [the king of Assyria] according to the slaughter of Midian at the rock of Oreb;[1] and as his rod was upon the sea so shall he lift it up after the manner of Egypt.

Isaiah promises the people that the day will come when their yoke and burden shall be removed, and the Lord will be the one who removes it. Of course, we know from history that one of the reasons the Jewish leaders in Jerusalem failed to recognize the Savior as their Messiah was because of their misunderstanding of Isaiah's promises in this regard. They looked forward to a leader who would militarily vanquish their enemies and be a strong political leader—in their case against Rome and Caesar.

Isaiah's teachings still have relevance for Nephi's record as a message to future generations of his own people, as well as to us today. Nephi wanted all of us to hear these words of warning against the dangers of having unrighteous leaders. He wanted to warn us all that an entire nation can go astray and fall into bondage because of bad leaders and false teachers. His warnings are perhaps even more appropriate today than at any other time in history. We see evidence of the truthfulness of these words daily on the news and in the papers. Not to be missed, however, is the adjunct to the warning that tells us, with the strongest testimony he could utter, that the Lord can fight our battles for us and he doesn't need armies to do it. All he requires of us is that we look to him and have faith in his teachings.

The Millennial Day

The next four chapters of Isaiah, as a group, contain a glorious prophecy about the Millennium, the events leading up to it, and the state of the people who are blessed to live during it. Each chapter takes a different aspect of the Millennium, and the state of the various people who will participate, or be present, at its advent. Chapter 11 of Isaiah (2 Nephi 21) talks about Jesus, both during his earthly ministry at the meridian of time, as well as his reign in the last days and throughout the millennium. Chapter 12 talks about the blessed condition of all men who get to stay and live during the millennium. Chapter 13 talks about the destruction of Babylon and all those who would fight against Zion, while chapter 14 talks about the house of Israel specifically, and their place in the kingdom at the last day.

Isaiah 11 and 2 Nephi 21

2 Nephi 21 contains one of the best descriptions of the Savior to be found in any scripture. The stem of Jesse, referred to in verse 1, refers to King David and the promise that the Savior would come through his lineage. David's father was Jesse and his line became the royal line of Israel. Though Israel would cease to have kings soon after David's son Solomon died, and the kingdom of Israel would be split apart, yet the people would forever hold on to the notion that the royal lineage of all of Israel belonged to David's family. The lineages of both Joseph and Mary are found in Matthew specifically to demonstrate that Jesus was born of this royal lineage, not just through God's lineage but through a worldly lineage as well (see Matthew 1).

> 1 And there shall come forth a rod out of the stem of Jesse, and a branch shall grow out of his roots.
> 2 And the Spirit of the Lord shall rest upon him, the spirit of wisdom and understanding, the spirit of counsel and might, the spirit of knowledge and of the fear of the Lord.
> 3 And shall make him quick of understanding in the fear of the Lord; and he shall not judge after the sight of his eyes, neither reprove after the hearing of his ears.

Verses 2 and 3 are a bit confusing because they talk about the spirit of the Lord and the fear of the Lord as if they are attributes of another being that the Savior was subject to. This is not an entirely false notion, for the Savior came to earth to do his Father's will and to speak for his Father. Numerous authorities, as well as the scriptures, have made the point that whether the Father or the Son says it, it is the same. The word *Spirit* is used four times in verse 2. Notice that "Spirit of the Lord" is the only time when the word *Spirit* is capitalized. Another term for the "Spirit of the Lord" is the "Holy Ghost." If we substitute "Holy Ghost" for "Spirit of the Lord" the verse makes more sense. It then says, "And the Holy Ghost shall rest upon him," which was, in fact, quite literally what happened at his baptism.

To say that the Savior was "quick of understanding" to the will of his Father would be an acceptable way of interpreting the reference to the "fear of the Lord" mentioned in verse 3. It should be noted here that the Old Testament prophets rarely, if ever, differentiated between Jehovah and Elohim. The name Elohim was so sacred, in fact, that it was only uttered by the priests, and even then only in the temple or synagogue on one special day of the year. It was at the time of the Savior's baptism that we first clearly see the three members of the Godhead as individual beings. We have the Savior standing in the water with John the Baptist, the Holy Ghost descending upon him in the form of a dove, and the Father's voice from heaven declaring, "This is my beloved Son in whom I am well pleased!" (Matthew 3:17). If we grant Isaiah some license for his sentence structure and word usage, these passages become clear and speak unmistakably about the Savior.

Verse 3 also makes an important point about the manner of the Lord's judgment that is worthy of mention here. Isaiah 11:3 says,

> 3 He shall not judge after the sight of his eyes, neither reprove after the hearing of his ears.

This brings to mind the statement from the Lord to Samuel where he said, "The Lord seeth not as man seeth; for man looketh on the outward appearance, but the Lord looketh on the heart" (1 Samuel 16:7). No other figure in biblical history could fit this description that Isaiah puts forth of Jesus.

Continuing the prophecy, Isaiah speaks of the Savior's compassion and love.

> 4 But with righteousness shall he judge the poor, and reprove with equity for the meek of the earth; and he shall smite the earth with the rod of his mouth, and with the breath of his lips shall he slay the wicked

5 And righteousness shall be the girdle of his loins, and faithfulness the girdle of his reins.

As this chapter continues, we see that Isaiah talks about all of the Lord's ministry and reign on earth as one event. Whether it be during his earthly ministry at the meridian of time, or during his triumphal return at the commencement of the Millennium, it is the same mission to Isaiah and he talks of the events as if they flow contiguously from one to the other. Verses 6–9 obviously speak of the peaceful condition of man and beast during the Millennium. However, verse 10 seems to speak of the reestablishment of the gospel in the latter days, preparatory to the Second Coming. When reading Isaiah 11, we need to understand this viewpoint of the all-in-one mission of the Savior. Verse 10 also marks the beginning of the prophecy that deals with the gathering of Israel in the last days.

10 And in that day there shall be a root of Jesse, which shall stand for an ensign of the people; to it shall the Gentiles seek, and his rest shall be glorious.

The reference to the Gentiles here suggest that they too will be eligible to be heirs with the Israelites in the glorious blessings of the gospel, including exaltation in the highest kingdom of our Father's domain. While we automatically understand and accept this concept today, we must realize that for a people who had been constantly told they were the chosen people and the seed of Abraham, the idea that they might have to share the celestial kingdom with the Gentiles was a very foreign and perhaps, even a distasteful thought.

Isaiah quickly moves on to the fate of the Israelites in the last days.

11 And it shall come to pass in that day that the Lord shall set his hand again the second time to recover the remnant of his people which shall be left, from Assyria, and from Egypt, and from Pathos, and from Cush, and from Elam, and from Shinar, and from Hamath, and from the isles of the sea.

12 And he shall set up an ensign for the nations, and shall assemble the outcasts of Israel, and gather together the dispersed of Judah from the four corners of the earth.

13 The envy of Ephraim also shall depart, and the adversaries of Judah shall be cut off; Ephraim shall not envy Judah, and Judah shall not vex Ephraim.

In other words, the whole house of Israel, or at least those that remain, will be gathered from wherever they may be scattered, along with the Gentiles who have sought the blessings of the gospel.

Isaiah 12 and 2 Nephi 22

2 Nephi 22 is a continuation of the grand vision Isaiah has laid out in chapter 21. In this chapter, however, he does not differentiate between ethnicities or factions. This is a demonstration of the reality that in that day all people who remain shall be of one mind and one heart. There will be no differences among them. There will be no more need to distinguish between the house of Judah and the House of Israel, or the Ephraimites, Assyrians, Nephites, Lamanites, or any other group into which we, as individuals, divide ourselves. All people who dwell in Zion will be one.

> 1 And in that day thou shalt say: O Lord, I will praise thee; though thou wast angry with me thine anger is turned away, and thou comfortedest me.
>
> 2 Behold, God is my salvation; I will trust, and not be afraid; for the Lord Jehovah is my strength and my song; he also has become my salvation.
>
> 3 Therefore, with joy shall ye draw waters out of the wells of salvation.
>
> 4 And in that day shall ye say: Praise the Lord, call upon his name, declare his doings among the people, make mention that his name is exalted.
>
> 5 Sing unto the Lord; for he hath done excellent things; this is known in all the earth.
>
> 6 Cry out and shout, thou inhabitants of Zion; for great is the Holy One of Israel in the midst of thee.

Notice that verse 4 says "his doings among the people." It does not say "his people," or "the chosen tribe"; it merely says "the people." In verse 6 they are called the "inhabitants of Zion." During mortality, people were divided into groups. Some were chosen to do one task and some to do another. The Lord would pronounce blessings or woe upon a people as a group rather than as individuals. The Millennium will be different. Wars will cease and differences between former enemies will fade. The lion and the lamb will lie down together, so it is reasonable to assume that animosities between peoples will disappear as well. Nations and tribes were originally formed to provide leadership and protection for a group of people. During the Millennium the Lord will be the royal leader and none will need protection because there will be no enemies. All those who would do harm will be disinvited from the event.

Isaiah 13 and 2 Nephi 23

One requirement for dwelling in Zion during the Millennium will be a loving heart and peaceful desires toward all men. For this reason, no scripture talks about people living during the Millennium without referring to them as a people of the Lord. His is the only kingdom that will survive. Those who would claim to be part of anything else have not come unto the Lord and will not be part of his millennial kingdom until they do. Thus we see in 2 Nephi 23, the awful state of those who refuse the Lord's offer of refuge from the worldly storm of mortality.

Chapter 23, which quotes Isaiah 13 word for word, refers to all the rebellious people of the earth as "Babylon." This is not referring particularly to those people who resided in the great city along the Euphrates River. Just as chapter 22 speaks of Zion as the place for all who dwell with the Lord, in chapter 23 Babylon is used to refer to the world and all those who refuse to give up worldly things. In the last days, as this dispensation culminates and the millennial dispensation unfolds, there will only be two people. They will either be the people of the Lord or the people against the Lord. Zion and Babylon will represent the Lord's kingdom and Lucifer's kingdom at the last day.

Verse 11 shows this idea clearly.

> 11 And I will punish the world for evil, and the wicked for their iniquity; I will cause the arrogancy of the proud to cease, and will lay down the haughtiness of the terrible.

In this verse the Lord says he will punish the world, not just a city or nation. He talks about the arrogance of the proud and the haughtiness of the terrible. He is talking about characteristics of people rather than nationalities or ethnicities.

Isaiah starts chapter 23 with the statement, "The burden of Babylon." The burden referred to is the inevitable consequence that follows sin. It is the weight of the sins of the world which will now cause it to fall. The wages of sin are a heavy burden to bear indeed, and we now see the price exacted by the Lord upon all those of every nation who esteemed his words as of little value.

6 Howl ye, for the day of the Lord is at hand; it shall come as a destruction from the Almighty.

7 Therefore shall all hands be faint; every man's heart shall melt;

8 And they shall be afraid; pangs and sorrows shall take hold of them; they shall be amazed one at another; their faces shall be as flames.

9 Behold, the day of the Lord cometh, cruel both with wrath and fierce anger, to lay the land desolate; and he shall destroy the sinners thereof out of it.

We have seen verses like this before during the warning to Israel, which we read about in the earlier chapters. These verses are different, however, because they are talking about those who fought against Israel and against the Lord. Previously, Isaiah was talking to the house of Judah specifically, because the Lord was wroth with her and would do what he needed to purify and cleanse her of wickedness. Now, however, Isaiah is talking about cleansing the rest of the world from wickedness. This chapter sounds like it should be included with those that were part of the warning instead of being in the section of chapters on hope. However, it is a very hopeful chapter because it is declaring that finally, after eons of wickedness and sin, the Lord is stepping in to put a stop to it. Those people who were and are righteous, with pure hearts and honest desires, will finally see the peace that has been promised for so long. This is a very exciting chapter because at last the bad guys get it, and it isn't going to be pretty.

14 And it shall be as the chased roe, and as the sheep that no man taketh up; and they shall every man turn to his own people, and flee every one into his own land.

15 Every one that is proud shall be thrust through; yea, and every one that is joined to the wicked shall fall by the sword.

16 Their children also shall be dashed to pieces before their eyes; their houses shall be spoiled and their wives ravished.

It is truly going to be awful for these people, and their fear and their embarrassment will be great. However, we must remember that these people are our brothers and sisters, and we should not gloat over their demise. Every spirit lost to Heavenly Father is a brother or sister we lose as well. Just as in the time of the flood, the heavens will surely weep for their loss. Nevertheless, we can take joy in the fact that the world will become a safe and peaceful place.

There are several lessons in Isaiah 13 and 2 Nephi 23. One is that in the world, sin is color blind. Throughout the Old Testament and the Book of Mormon we continually see that people on either side of a conflict were equally capable of wickedness. The house of Israel was seldom any more righteous than those who vexed them. The Nephites became more evil and more corrupt than the Lamanites ever were. The Lord protected one group or another, even though they were steeped in wickedness, not because he was turning a blind eye to their wickedness, nor because they were special somehow, but because, as a people, they had a calling and a work to perform upon the earth.

Though the Israelites and the Nephites were, at times, subject to bouts of unfaithfulness, as a people they had the calling of perpetuating the gospel throughout the world. In the Old World it was the house of Judah through whom the Savior would come, and it is the testimonies of their prophets that we cherish today as the Bible. In the New World it was the Nephites who would keep the records and the history of their people, wicked though they may have been, to provide a testimony and a second witness of Jesus Christ for us. The Book of Mormon prophets must have felt exactly like the Old Testament prophets as they watched their people become mired in sin and wickedness. Nevertheless, their people were preserved at least as long as it took to accomplish their assigned tasks. As a result, the gospel is upon the earth today, and we have the Bible and the Book of Mormon.

Isaiah 14 and 2 Nephi 24

Chapter 14 of Isaiah is the culminating chapter of this long run of Isaiah that Nephi has included in his record. He will, after a few more chapters of commentary, include Isaiah 29, but that is from a different section of Isaiah's works and it stands alone in its unique message. This chapter, found in 2 Nephi 24, finishes off the four chapter "apocalyptic writings" of Isaiah. We have seen the prophecy of Jesus' earthly ministry and his millennial reign. We have read about the blessed state of those who get to reside with the Lord during that reign. Isaiah has shown us the awful state of those who have fought against the Lord and have rejected his word, and we have seen what is to become of them. Now, finally, we will see what is to become of the house of Israel.

In 2 Nephi 24 we read Isaiah's prophecies about the final state of Israel. We see that Israel will finally grow to become the repository for and the guardians of the kingdom of the Lord. Lucifer will be cast out and Israel (or the Lord's kingdom) will triumph over Babylon (or the world) and the devil's kingdom.

> 1 For the Lord will have mercy on Jacob, and will yet choose Israel, and set them in their own land; and the strangers shall be joined with them, and they shall cleave to the house of Jacob.

In other words, even though Israel has been a challenging group for the Lord, even though she has been disobedient like a little child that disobeys her parents, she is still part of the family. Israel still belongs to the Lord. The Lord will be merciful and, in the end, Israel will get to dwell in her promised land. Isaiah 14 says that strangers will be joined to her. This hearkens back to the blessings the Lord gave Abraham wherein he said that all those who would come to the Lord would only be able to do so through Abraham's descendants. Abraham was told that all who accepted the gospel would become his children and would call him father (Abraham 2:10). Here, Isaiah is saying that this promise is in full force and effect. He says the strangers will join them and cleave to the house of Jacob.

The house of Jacob will finally have the king they have sought all along, and they will finally understand how he is to lead them.

> 3 And it shall come to pass in that day that the Lord shall give thee rest, from thy sorrow, and from thy fear, and from the hard bondage wherein thou wast made to serve.
> 4 And it shall come to pass in that day, that thou shalt take up this proverb against the king of Babylon, and say: How hath the oppressor ceased, the golden city ceased!
> 5 The Lord hath broken the staff of the wicked, the scepters of the rulers. . . .
> 7 The whole earth is at rest, and is quiet; they break forth into singing.

Peace will finally be restored to Israel through the Lord's hand. Isaiah then uses some interesting imagery to show how the kingdoms of the world will fare. He says:

> 9 Hell from beneath is moved for thee to meet thee at thy coming; it stirreth up the dead for thee, even all the chief ones of the earth; it hath raised up from their thrones all the kings of the nations.
> 10 And they shall speak and say unto thee; Art thou also become weak as we? Art thou become like unto us?

The implication of these verses is that all the kings and other powerful worldly leaders belong to Lucifer's kingdom and that their final resting place is in hell. Verse 9 says hell "hath raised up from their thrones all the kings of the nations." Just prior to that it says it "stirreth up the dead," so by inference we understand that the final seats of power, or "thrones," of the kings are in hell. In other words, notwithstanding all the talk through the ages about "Divine Right" and "Holy empires," kings were generally sustained in power through terror and bloodshed. They bowed to a god, to be sure, but it was usually the "god of this world," who is identified in the scriptures as Satan (2 Corinthians 4:4). According to verse 10 they shall come to see the emptiness of their power and will look with envy upon those righteous individuals who become heirs of all the Father has.

As Isaiah continues this passage, he shows that not only will kings be brought down but their god as well. It is then that we realize that the "thee" to whom they speak in verse 10, who has become weak like the kings, is in fact Lucifer himself. Verse 12 addresses Lucifer saying:

> 12 How art thou fallen from heaven, O Lucifer, son of the morning! Art thou cut down to the ground, which did weaken the nations!

Isaiah here demonstrates that it was Lucifer who weakened the nations of man and that he, as the god of this world, is no more immune to the judgments of the Lord than are the kings of the earth.

This final chapter then gives us one of the clearest revelations of Lucifer's original scheme and plot against the Father that is found in all of the scriptures. He says, starting in verse 13:

> 13 For thou hast said in thy heart, I will ascend into heaven, I will exalt my throne above the stars of God; I will sit upon the mount of the congregation, in the sides of the north;
> 14 I will ascend above the heights of the clouds; I will be like the Most High.

We can only guess what kind of arrogance and pride could have caused this son of the morning to turn so avaricious and greedy in the premortal life. It is clear from Isaiah's text that his plan was to usurp God and sit upon his throne, to "be like the Most High." As we read these words and contemplate their message, it becomes apparent that the common Christian view of hell as being a place where Satan reigns is unsustainable throughout the eternities. While it is true, and we are taught, that Satan will have power over this earth for a time, it would be illogical to think that hell would be his personal domain and kingdom for all time. If we, as spirits and as humans, are to be judged according to our works, it would hold that he who was the most wicked, or who did the least amount of good works would be at the bottom of the reward list in the end. Rather than being Lord of the underworld throughout eternity, he would be its lowest denizen; its least glorious inhabitant. And so it is that Isaiah continues with the description of Lucifer's ignominious final state.

15 Yet thou shall be brought down to hell, to the sides of the pit.

16 They that see thee shall narrowly look upon thee, and shall consider thee, and shall say: Is this the man that made the earth to tremble, that did shake the kingdoms?

17 And made the world as a wilderness and destroyed the cities thereof, and opened not the house of his prisoners?

18 All the kings of the nations, yea, all of them, lie in glory, every one of them in his own house.

19 But thou art cast out of thy grave like an abominable branch, and the remnant of those that are slain, thrust through with a sword, that go down to the stones of the pit; as a carcass trodden under feet.

20 Thou shalt not be joined with them in burial, because thou hast destroyed thy land and slain thy people; the seed of evil-doers shall never be renowned.

Verse 16 says that in that day when Lucifer is put down, we will look upon him narrowly or with little regard. We will be amazed to see this now powerless being and marvel that he was once able to wreak so much havoc and horror upon all the generations of man. Isaiah then says that Lucifer will not even occupy a place as high as the kings of the earth who once served him. This is consistent with the doctrine that says only those with a particularly special witness and knowledge of the truth can be eligible for perdition, or outer darkness. Lucifer chose evil over good, and he did so with great knowledge and understanding of the Father's plan. Because of this, he is fated to spend eternity in perdition, or outer darkness, wherein there is not a whit of glory. The kings of the earth who served him had no such knowledge, and as such, they have claim to some of the mercies of the Savior. They can eventually be reclaimed to one degree or another and verse 18 states that they will have some degree of glory. Each will have his own house, as the Lord said, "In my Father's kingdom are many mansions. . . . I go to prepare a place for you" (John 14:2).

This section of Isaiah ends with Isaiah giving his version of the scripture which says that every knee shall bow and every tongue confess that Jesus is the Christ. He says:

> 32 What shall then answer the messengers of the nations? That the
> Lord hath founded Zion, and the poor of his people shall trust in it.

In other words, all will know that the Lord rules and reigns over this
fantastic city of Zion. He is saying that everyone will know and acknowledge it. This is a fitting end for the writings of Isaiah, as transcribed by
Nephi and Mormon and translated by Joseph Smith. These thirteen chapters have pretty well covered the entire range of history and experience for
the house of Israel and its various factions. Isaiah's prophecies began by
reminding the Israelites of just who they were and what their purpose was
on behalf of the Lord. Their sins were revealed and dire warnings were
given to persuade them to turn to righteousness. They were instructed on
the nature of politics and the inherent weaknesses of worldly leaders. They
were told that through the unrighteousness of their own leaders they would
be conquered and vanquished. Prophecies showed them how they would be
driven out of the land of their inheritance and made to wander from place
to place. They were told about the Savior and his healing power, offered
freely to all who would accept him. They were shown the great events leading up to the culminating last days of the mortal world, and they were given
to hear the awful fate of those who chose not to follow the Lord. Finally,
they were shown the blessed state of those who dwelt with the Lord during
the Millennium, while at the same time they saw the ignominious end of
those who spent their lives fighting against the Lord.

Every word recorded by Nephi in this section had relevance to the
Nephites, their brethren the Lamanites, and us today. Of this fact Nephi
clearly bore testimony in his next chapter. Speaking of why he wrote the
words of Isaiah he said:

> For I know that they shall be of great worth unto them in the last
> days; for in that day shall they understand them; wherefore, for their
> good have I written them. (2 Nephi 25:8)

Nephi uses chapter 25 and 26 to record his own prophecy concerning Israel and his people, the descendents of Lehi, in the New World.
He explains that the words of Isaiah are hard for his people to understand because they have not been taught in the manner of speaking of the
Jews. However, he has lived in Jerusalem and he is well-educated in their
manner. Building upon the words of Isaiah, which he has just recorded, he

can now record his own prophecy. In contrast to Isaiah's words, Nephi's words are clear and simple to understand. He speaks very directly and to the point, always tying his words back to Isaiah. In chapter 25, verse 7 and the beginning of verse 8 show this clearly.

> 7 But behold, I proceed with mine own prophecy, according to my plainness; in the which I know that no man can err; nevertheless, in the days that the prophecies of Isaiah shall be fulfilled men shall know of a surety, at the times when they shall come to pass.
>
> 8 Wherefore, they are of worth unto the children of men, and he that supposeth that they are not, unto him will I speak particularly, and confine the words unto mine own people;

By using Isaiah as a foundation for his own prophecies, Nephi has established a credibility for his own words that cannot be denied. It must have been easy for many of the people to think that by leaving Jerusalem and establishing themselves on a new continent they would have escaped the fate and destiny of the house of Israel. Nephi's use of the written record of Isaiah, however, could leave no doubt that Isaiah's prophecies were addressed to the whole house of Israel wherever they were found, including the isles of the sea. This was important to establish so that the Nephites would have sufficient esteem and honor for the law and the teachings that Nephi brought with him from Jerusalem. Had he not been able to do this, the Nephites would probably have ended up like the Mulekites.

We have just finished the largest excerpt of Isaiah found in the Book Of Mormon. It is often skipped over by impatient readers. One reason for skipping it is because of the extraordinary prophecy that comes immediately after it. The prophecy that Nephi utters concerning the last days is compelling reading to be sure, but those who gain an understanding of Isaiah's teaching and understand that Nephi wanted Isaiah to provide his introduction will come away with a greater understanding of what Nephi had to say.

Notes

1. The slaughter of Midian at the rock of Oreb refers to the biblical story of Gideon (Judges 7–8), which all good Israelites would surely have known. Gideon whittled down his troops to just three hundred men, who he then led into battle against Midian. In the battle (which Gideon's troops ultimately won) they captured two of Midian's princes, one being Oreb, who was killed at the rock of Oreb.

6

"A Book that Is Sealed"

After using sections of the book of Isaiah to set up his own prophecy concerning the future of the world, Nephi delivered some very powerful and very plainly spoken words about the future of his own people on the American continents. He says in 2 Nephi 25:20: "And now my brethren, I have spoken plainly that ye cannot err."

He laid out precisely the course of events that would transpire over the balance of the Nephite history. He foretold, in 2 Nephi 26, the crucifixion and resurrection of the Savior and the signs that would be delivered to the Nephites and the Lamanites concerning those events. He prophesied of the Savior's appearance to the people of the New World but warned that the unity and peace that ensued would only last a few generations and then destruction would come.

As Nephi's prophecy continued, he touched upon the legacy that his people would leave to future generations in the form of their writings. He said:

> 16 For those who shall be destroyed shall speak to them out of the ground, and their speech shall be low out of the dust, and their voice shall be as one that hath a familiar spirit; for the Lord God will give unto him power, that he may whisper concerning them, even as it were out of the ground; and their speech shall whisper out of the dust.
>
> 17 For thus saith the Lord God: They shall write the things which shall be done among them, and they shall be written and sealed up in a book, and those who have dwindled in unbelief shall not have them, for they seek to destroy the things of God.

It was this part of Nephi's prophecy that led him to return to Isaiah one more time. He recalled Isaiah's prophecy about the turbulent last days and about an ancient sealed book that would come forth in the last days.

It might be tempting to think of 2 Nephi 27 as a continuation of the larger excerpt of Isaiah we have just studied. After all, it comes just two chapters later in Nephi's record. However, the section we have just finished was comprised of Isaiah 2–14, which formed an extensive and complete prophecy about the condition of the kingdoms of Israel and Judah throughout the ages, including the Millennium. We are now looking at Isaiah 29, a chapter that falls fifteen chapters later in Isaiah's record and which contains its own unique prophecy and message.

Isaiah 29 is a prophecy about a book that is slated to come forth in the latter days—the Book of Mormon. The prophecy is unique, because it is found in the very book it is prophesying about. It must be remembered that the Book of Mormon did not exist when Isaiah wrote this prophecy, nor when Nephi decided to include it in his own personal record. Logic would tell us that Mormon, or even Moroni for that matter, would have been more inclined to include Isaiah 29 as an addendum or an appendix to their compilation. They could have used it to show the special nature and calling of the Book of Mormon. Instead, it was Nephi who included it as part of the expansive prophecy he was delivering concerning the rise and fall of his own people.

As we begin our study of 2 Nephi 27, it is important to note that this is the only time in all of Nephi's record and teachings that he does not specifically attribute the words to Isaiah. He does not say, "For the prophet Isaiah hath said" or "and now I return unto the words of the prophet Isaiah," or some such introduction as he has each time in the past. Nephi has been delivering a powerful prophecy of his own concerning the future course of events of his people, during which he has foretold of their total destruction. His prophecy led him to the fact that they would leave a record of their destruction and that this record would "whisper out of the dust" and speak as one that "hath a familiar spirit." Chapter 27 speaks of that book and Nephi continues right on from chapters 25 and 26 without pause.

One reasonable explanation for not citing Isaiah as the author of chapter 27 could be that these words may not have been taken from his written text of Isaiah. Rather, they could have been part of a revelation given to him personally. The fact that Nephi could have had the same vision as Isaiah is not so unusual when we consider that a prophecy contains truth, and truth does not change over time.

Numerous examples of different prophets receiving the same vision exist throughout the scriptures. Indeed, the great apocalyptic vision of the world from beginning to end seems to be a pretty standard revelation. In our own scriptures we have accounts of that particular vision from Enoch, Moses, Abraham, Isaiah, John the Revelator, Nephi, and Mormon. All had the same vision and all were instructed to record various parts of it. Nephi was instructed to limit his record of it by the following commandment found in 1 Nephi 14:

> But the things which thou shalt see hereafter thou shalt not write; for the Lord God hath ordained the apostle of the Lamb of God that he should write them.
>
> And also others who have been, to them hath he shown all things, and they have written them; and they are sealed up to come forth in their purity, according to the truth which is in the Lamb, in the own due time of the Lord, unto the house of Israel. (vv. 25–26)

Latter-day scholars of the Book of Mormon included the note "compare Isaiah 29" in the heading of this chapter, and the comparison is certainly valid. However, 2 Nephi 27 is the most dramatic departure from the word-for-word style of citing a biblical prophet in the Book of Mormon. In the same way that Moroni expanded upon Malachi's words when he visited Joseph Smith three times in one night, Nephi gives a greatly expanded and much clearer version of the "sealed book" prophecy than is contained in the written record of Isaiah. (This is not to say that Isaiah did not originally have the same vision or write the same words.) Whatever the truth may be, Nephi's version of this particular vision is unmistakably clear.

For the purpose of comparison, we will place the two texts side by side with 2 Nephi 27 on the left and Isaiah 29 on the right, but first we should take a look at verse 1 in Nephi's account. This verse does not appear in Isaiah.

> 1 But, behold, in the last days, or in the days of the Gentiles—yea, behold all the nations of the Gentiles and also the Jews, both those who shall come upon this land and those who shall be on other lands, yea, even upon all the lands of the earth, behold, they will be drunken with iniquity and all manner of abominations.

According to Nephi there were to be dark times "in the days of the Gentiles." Iniquity and abominations would abound in all the nations of the earth. When Joseph Smith knelt in the Sacred Grove and sought guidance from God as to which church he should join, he was told to join none of them, as they were all false to one degree or another. Starting with the next verse, both Nephi and Isaiah continue the bleak exposition of the times. The verse numbering is different for the same texts.

2 Nephi 27:2–5	Isaiah 29: 6–10

2 **And when that day shall come they** shall be visited of the Lord of Hosts, with thunder and with earthquake, and with **a** great noise, and with storm, and with tempest, and **with** the flame of devouring fire.

3 And all the nations that fight against Zion, and that distress her, shall be as a dream of a night vision; yea, it shall be **unto them**, even as unto a hungry man which dreameth, and behold he eateth but he awaketh and his soul is empty; **or like unto** a thirsty man **which** dreameth, and behold he drinketh but he awaketh and behold he is faint, and his soul hath appetite; yea, **even** so shall the multitude of all the nations be that fight against Mount Zion.

4 **For behold, all ye that doeth iniquity**, stay yourselves and wonder, for **ye shall** cry out, and cry; yea, **ye shall be** drunken but not with wine, **ye shall** stagger but not with strong drink.

5 For **behold**, the Lord hath poured out upon you the spirit of deep sleep. **For behold, ye** have closed your eyes, **and ye have rejected** the prophets; and your rulers, **and** the seers hath he covered **because of your iniquity**.

6 Thou shalt be visited of the Lord of hosts with thunder, and with earthquake, and with great noise, with storm and with tempest, and the flame of devouring fire.

7 And **the multitude of** all the nations that fight against **Ariel, even all that fight against her and her munition**, and that distress her, shall be as a dream of a night vision.

8 It shall even be as when an hungry man dreameth, and, behold, he eateth; but he awaketh, and his soul is empty: or as **when** a thirsty man dreameth, and, behold, he drinketh; but he awaketh, and, behold, he is faint, and his soul hath appetite: so shall **the multitude of** all the nations be, that fight against mount Zion.

9 Stay yourselves, and wonder; cry ye out, and cry: they are drunken, but not with wine; they stagger, but not with strong drink.

10 For the Lord hath poured out upon you the spirit of deep sleep, and hath closed your eyes: the prophets and your rulers, the seers hath he covered.

Here, as in the early examples of Isaiah's text, we see that a few clarifying words significantly ease the understanding of the scripture. Nephi's purer text narrows the focus of the prophecies to "all ye that doeth iniquity." In verse 5, for example, the Lord does not capriciously cause a deep sleep or close the eyes of the prophets, rather, he says, we cause those things to happen because "ye have rejected the prophets . . . because of your iniquity." Once again we see that without the clearer text of the Book of Mormon, the Bible would have us believe that the Lord acts unilaterally and without cause. This seems to be a most unfortunate legacy of the Old Testament translators, but it correctly reflects the attitudes about God and punishment that existed during the Middle Ages.

Now we get to the scriptures that foretell the coming forth of the Book of Mormon and the events that surround its arrival. It is here that Nephi's vision, or at least his written account of the vision, has a great deal more detail and substance than Isaiah's record.

Verse 11 of Isaiah 29 is expanded to a text of at least 12 verses in 2 Nephi. The difference is impressive when the two accounts are placed side by side.

2 Nephi 27:6–18

6 And it shall come to pass that the Lord God shall bring forth unto you the words of a book, and they shall be the words of them which have slumbered.

7 And behold the book shall be sealed; and in the book shall be a revelation from God, from the beginning of the world to the ending thereof.

8 Wherefore, because of the things which are sealed up, the things which are sealed shall not be delivered in the day of the wickedness and abominations of the people. Wherefore the book shall be kept from them.

9 But the book shall be delivered unto a man, and he shall deliver the words of the book, which are the

Isaiah 29:11

11 And the vision of all is become unto you as the words of a book

that is sealed,

words of those who have slumbered in the dust, and he shall deliver these words unto another;

10 But the words which are sealed he shall not deliver, neither shall he deliver the book. For the book shall be sealed by the power of God, and the revelation which was sealed shall be kept in the book until the own due time of the Lord, that they may come forth; for behold, they reveal all things from the foundation of the world unto the end thereof.

11 And the day cometh that the words of the book which were sealed shall be read upon the house tops; and they shall be read by the power of Christ; and all things shall be revealed unto the children of men which ever have been among the children of men, and which ever will be even unto the end of the earth.

12 Wherefore, at that day when the book shall be delivered unto the man of whom I have spoken, the book shall be hid from the eyes of the world, that the eyes of none shall behold it save it be that three witnesses shall behold it, by the power of God, besides him to whom the book shall be delivered; and they shall testify to the truth of the book and the things therein.

13 And there is none other which shall view it, save it be a few according to the will of God, to bear testimony of his word unto the children of men; for the Lord God hath said that the words of the faithful should speak as if it were from the dead.

14 Wherefore, the Lord God will proceed to bring forth the words of

the book; and in the mouth of as many witnesses as seemeth him good will he establish his word; and wo be unto him that rejecteth the word of God!

15 But behold, it shall come to pass that the Lord God shall say unto him to whom he shall deliver the book: Take these words which are not sealed and deliver them to another, that he may show them unto the learned, saying: Read this, I pray thee. And the learned shall say: Bring hither the book, and I will read them.

16 And now, because of the glory of the world and to get gain will they say this, and not for the glory of God.

17 And the man shall say: I cannot bring the book, for it is sealed.

18 Then shall the learned say: I cannot read it.

which men deliver unto one that

is learned, saying, Read this, I pray thee,

And he saith, I cannot, for it is sealed.

It should come as no surprise that Nephi's version of this prophecy would be richer in detail than Isaiah's, for to Nephi this was a prophecy about his own people and his own written words. He had seen in a vision, and so testified, that his words would go forth unto the future generations in the latter days, so it is no wonder that he would strive to record as complete a text of this vision as possible. So too would Mormon be sure to keep this prophecy intact as he diligently labored through his editing process nearly a thousand years later.

The book that Isaiah had seen in his vision was the Book of Mormon. Of that there can be no doubt. There is not even the suggestion of any other book in the entire world history that could come close to claiming to be the sealed book of Isaiah's vision.

Perhaps more important, no other book in the world has ever attempted to lay claim to that distinction, and no man has ever claimed to possess one. And yet, Isaiah clearly said a book would come forth in the latter days. He said that it would be sealed and that it would be delivered to a learned man who would say, "I cannot read a sealed book."

On the other hand, an account of the literal fulfillment of this very event exists in Church history. It is the account of Professor Charles Anthon—a scholar in ancient languages at Columbia University to whom Martin Harris delivered a copy of the hieroglyphs as translated by Joseph Smith. Joseph records the following:

> I commenced copying the characters off the plates. I copied a con- siderable number of them, and by means of the Urim and Thummim I translated them. Mr. Harris came to our place, got the characters which I had drawn off the plates and started with them to the city of New York. For what took place relative to him and the characters I refer to his own account of the circumstances as he related them to me after his return, which was as follows; "I went to the city of New York and presented the characters that had been translated, with the translation thereof, to Professor Charles Anthon, a gentleman celebrated for his literary attainments. Professor Anthon stated that the translation was correct, more so than any he had seen previously from the Egyptian. I then showed him those that were not yet translated and he said that they were Egyptian, Chaldean, Assyrian, and Arabic; and he said they were true characters. He gave me a certificate, certifying to the people of Palmyra that they were true characters, and that the translation of such as had been translated was also correct. I took the certificate and put it into my pocket, and was just leaving the house, when Mr. Anthon called me back and asked me how the young man found out there were gold plates in the place where he found them. I answered that an angel of God had revealed it unto him.
>
> He then said to me: "Let me see that certificate." I accordingly took it out of my pocket and gave it back to him, when he took it and tore it in pieces, saying, that there was no such thing now as minister- ing angels, and that if I would bring the plates to him, he would trans- late them. I informed him that part of the plates were sealed, and that I was forbidden to bring them. He replied, "I cannot read a sealed book." I left him and went to Dr. Mitchell, who sanctioned what Professor Anthon had said respecting both the characters and the translation.[1]

This exchange took place in February 1828. Though Professor Anthon later tried to deny that the event ever took place, he did acknowledge Martin Harris's visit. It should be noted that Martin Harris was suffi- ciently impressed with Professor Anthon's initial reaction to the charac- ters and their translation that he returned to Joseph Smith and continued to assist in the work of bringing forth the Book of Mormon. He even provided three thousand dollars of his own money, a very sizeable sum in those days, for the publication of the first edition and initial run of five thousand copies of the book when it was completed!

Other promises contained in Nephi's version are completely missing from the Isaiah text. They include verses 12 through 14, which speak of witnesses to the Book of Mormon. Indeed, the Lord did direct Joseph Smith to have three men assemble to see for themselves the gold plates. Oliver Cowdery, David Whitmer, and Martin Harris were privileged to have the angel Moroni himself present the gold plates to them and allow them to touch them. Their testimony, which appears at the beginning of the Book of Mormon, says in part:

> And we declare with words of soberness, that an angel of God came down from heaven, and he brought and laid before our eyes, that we beheld and saw the plates, and the engravings thereon; and we know that it is by the grace of God the Father, and our Lord Jesus Christ, that we beheld and bear record that these things are true.[2]

Oliver, David, and Martin were able to handle the plates and converse with the angel Moroni about them. They were selected by God to be the three special witnesses referred to by Nephi in verse 12. Their testimony stands witness to all the world and to those who read the Book of Mormon that it is true and that it is authentic. Each of these men suffered throughout his life for the testimony he gave of the Book of Mormon, yet each remained steadfast and true to his words to the end of his life.

Verses 13 and 14 mention a few other witnesses that the Lord might call as he saw fit, and in these same introductory pages, we find the testimony of eight other men who were privileged to view the plates. Four other members of David Whitmer's family along with Hiram Page and three members of Joseph Smith's family were allowed to enter a room where the plates were sitting on a table. They did not see nor were they addressed by the angel Moroni. They were, however, allowed to touch the plates and feel their texture and weight. Their testimony stands through the eternities along with that of the three special witnesses that the Book of Mormon is true and authentic. Their testimony says in part:

> We did handle with our hands; and we also saw the engravings thereon, all of which has the appearance of ancient workmanship. And this we bear record with words of soberness, that the said Smith has

shown unto us, for we have seen and hefted, and know of a surety that the said Smith has got the plates of which we have spoken.[3]

After uttering the prophecy fulfilled by the Professor Anthon episode, Nephi takes occasion to expand upon Isaiah's record with the next verse. Isaiah 29:12 is short and simple with a mere 24 words. Nephi's text expands that to seven verses.

2 Nephi 27:19	Isaiah 29:12
19 **Wherefore it shall come to pass, that the Lord God will** deliver again the book **and the words thereof** to him that is not learned; and the man that is not learned shall say: I am not learned.	12 And the book is delivered to him that is not learned, saying, Read this, I pray thee: and he saith, I am not learned.

20 Then shall the Lord God say unto him: The learned shall not read them, for they have rejected them, and I am able to do mine own work; wherefore thou shalt read the words which I shall give unto thee.

21 Touch not the things which are sealed, for I will bring them forth in mine own due time; for I will show unto the children of men that I am able to do mine own work.

22 Wherefore, when thou hast read the words which I have commanded thee, and obtained the witnesses which I have promised unto thee, then shalt thou seal up the book again, and hide it up unto me, that I may preserve the words which thou hast not read, until I shall see fit in mine own wisdom to reveal all things unto the children of men.

23 For behold, I am God; and I am a God of miracles; and I will show unto the world that I am the same yesterday, today, and forever; and I work

not among the children of men save it be according to their faith.

24 And again it shall come to pass that the Lord shall say unto him that shall read the words that shall be delivered him:

These verses give instructions to Joseph Smith with regard to the handling of the sealed portion of the Book of Mormon. Joseph stated that approximately one-third of the gold plates were sealed with a gold band around them, preventing him from seeing their content.

At this point, Isaiah 29 picks back up and the two texts deliver a similar message. They both continue the thought that was started with 2 Nephi 27:24.

2 Nephi 27:25–26	Isaiah 29:13–14
25 Forasmuch as this people draw near **unto** me with their mouth, and with their lips do honor me, but have removed their hearts far from me, and their fear towards me is taught by the precepts of men—	13 **Wherefore the Lord said,** Forasmuch as this people draw near me with their mouth, and with their lips do honour me, but have removed their heart far from me, and their fear toward me is taught by the precept of men:
26 Therefore, I will proceed to do a marvelous work among this people, **yea**, a marvelous work and a wonder, for the wisdom of their wise **and learned** shall perish, and the understanding of their prudent shall be hid.	14 Therefore, **behold**, I will proceed to do a marvellous work among this people, even a marvellous work and a wonder: for the wisdom of their wise **men** shall perish, and the understanding of their prudent **men** shall be hid.

These verses speak to the loss of knowledge among the children of men that would exist in the latter days. Because there was no revelation and no prophet to keep the doctrine correct, the task of maintaining correct interpretation of scripture fell to the learned and wise men of the various churches. It would be unfair to condemn all such men as evil or foolish. Instead, we should realize that many church leaders did the best they could with limited understanding of oft-times confusing scriptures. We have shown in this work that the biblical records of such prophets as Isaiah were sometimes less than complete and always very difficult to understand. We have seen how the addition of just a few words here and there can sometimes make a huge difference. Without such clarifications, confusion would be the natural result of devoted study, and differences of opinion would surely arise. This is not to say that there were not, nor are not, men of conspiring designs within many churches. It is presented merely to point out that men, left to their own understanding and judgment, will generally make less than perfect assumptions and interpretations of the things of God.

Verse 25 makes the point that people in the latter days would often say the right things because of an intellectual and studied knowledge but without the fulness of understanding, their hearts could not really get into the spirit of the doctrine. As a result, most people's fear (respect) of God would be based on teachings, sometimes false and misleading, which, because they were not pure and true, would cause confusion. It is impossible for the Holy Ghost to bear witness to something that is not true; therefore, as more and more doctrine became corrupted, the Holy Ghost had less and less to testify about in the hearts of men.

The marvelous work and wonder that the Lord was about to bring forth was the restoration of the truth and the fulness of the gospel through a humble uneducated boy of tender age. God needed a young and uneducated boy with a sincere heart so that he could work from a clean slate, as it were, planting truths in his mind and allowing the Holy Ghost to burn those truths into his heart. The wonder was that these truths would ultimately put down and wash away so many false notions and shed such light on the hearts and minds of those humble enough to seriously consider them. This restored knowledge would miraculously give new meaning to age-old questions about life such as "Where did I come from," "Why am I here," and "Where am I going?" As people find these truths, and find purpose for their lives, the effect is marvelous and wonderful.

This restored truth would have another effect on the children of men. With the truth comes a washing away of excuses to do wrong. Men could no longer hide behind ignorance and myth to justify their evil and wicked ways. False priests and teachers could no longer twist the doctrine to fit their needs, and they could no longer enrich themselves with impunity through false teachings and coercion of the ignorant followers. Of such men the next few verses speak.

2 Nephi 27:27–28

27 And wo unto them that seek deep to hide their counsel from the Lord! And their works are in the dark; and they say: Who seeth us, and who knoweth us? **And they also say**: Surely, your turning of things upside down shall be esteemed as the potter's clay. **But behold, I will show unto them, saith the Lord of Hosts, that I know all their works**. For shall the work say of him that made it, he made me not? Or shall the thing framed say of him that framed it, he had no understanding?

28 **But behold, saith the Lord of Hosts: I will show unto the children of men that it is** yet a very little while and Lebanon shall be turned into a fruitful field; and the fruitful field shall be esteemed as a forest.

Isaiah 29:15–17

15 Woe unto them that seek deep to hide their counsel from the Lord, and their works are in the dark, and they say, Who seeth us? and who knoweth us?

16 Surely your turning of things upside down shall be esteemed as the potter's clay:

for shall the work say of him that made it, He made me not? or shall the thing framed say of him that framed it, He had no understanding?

17 Is it not yet a very little while, and Lebanon shall be turned into a fruitful field, and the fruitful field shall be esteemed as a forest?

These verses indicate that when truth breaks forth, evil and falsehood will be harder to sustain, and every man will be held accountable for the work of his own hands. No more will people be justified in claiming ignorance of the truth as an excuse for their acts; rather, all things will have to stand the test of truth to prevail.

Nephi and Isaiah both attribute this great change to the book which will come forth providing truth to all men. They say:

2 Nephi 27:29–30

29 And in that day shall the deaf hear the words of the book, **and** the eyes of the blind shall see out of obscurity and out of **the** darkness.

30 And the meek also shall increase, **and** their joy **shall be** in the Lord, and the poor among men shall rejoice in the Holy One of Israel.

Isaiah 29:18–19

18 And in that day shall the deaf hear the words of the book, and the eyes of the blind shall see out of obscurity, and out of darkness.

19 The meek also shall increase their joy in the Lord, and the poor among men shall rejoice in the Holy One of Israel.

The deafness here referred to is the inability to find and hear the truth. This scripture says that this will no longer be the case. No longer will men be blinded by their inability to find the truth. It will be present for all who choose to see. The scriptures also promise that those who humbly endeavor to follow the Lord in the best manner they know how will no longer be made to feel ashamed by the proud and wicked men of the world. No longer will they have to withstand the mocking and derision of those whose pride and vanity is based purely on worldly things. Instead, they will rejoice because of the increased knowledge that will flow down from heaven and because of the words of truth as provided by the book. What a wonderful book this will be for those who have humbly and diligently sought for the truth. And at the same time, what a scourge to the wicked, and a condemnation of the evil who, heretofore, were able to hide behind ignorance and the dearth of light and knowledge which existed among the children of men.

The next few verses promise that the consequence of this book coming forth will be profound for the evil men of the world.

Nephi 27:31–32	Isaiah 29:20–21
31 **For assuredly as the Lord liveth they shall see that** the terrible one is brought to naught, and the scorner is consumed, and all that watch for iniquity are cut off;	20 For the terrible one is brought to nought, and the scorner is consumed, and all that watch for iniquity are cut off:
32 **And they** that make a man an offender for a word, and lay a snare for him that reproveth in the gate, and turn aside the just for a thing of naught.	21 That make a man an offender for a word, and lay a snare for him that reproveth in the gate, and turn aside the just for a thing of nought.

Without the truth there is really no effective way to put down the evil man. How is judgment brought to bear? How is justice served if judgment and justice are ill-defined and variable according to the precepts of men? With the establishment of truth, as witnessed by the Holy Ghost and supported by the Lord through a living prophet, judgment and justice are fixed and immutable. It is only then that the wicked and evil men of the world can be brought down.

Finally, with the last few verses of this chapter, we see the fulfilling of the promises that the Father made to Abraham concerning his posterity and the future house of Israel. The promise is made in these last verses that Israel will be redeemed and its people will come to a knowledge of the truth.

2 Nephi 27:33–35

33 Therefore, thus saith the Lord, who redeemed Abraham, concerning the house of Jacob: Jacob shall not now be ashamed, neither shall his face now wax pale.

34 But when he seeth his children, the work of my hands, in the midst of him, they shall sanctify my name, and sanctify the Holy One of Jacob, and shall fear the God of Israel.

35 They also that erred in spirit shall come to understanding, and they that murmured shall learn doctrine.

Isaiah 29:22–24

22 Therefore thus saith the Lord, who redeemed Abraham, concerning the house of Jacob, Jacob shall not now be ashamed, neither shall his face now wax pale.

23 But when he seeth his children, the work of mine hands, in the midst of him, they shall sanctify my name, and sanctify the Holy One of Jacob, and shall fear the God of Israel.

24 They also that erred in spirit shall come to understanding, and they that murmured shall learn doctrine.

The visions and prophecies that both Isaiah and Nephi left us concerning the coming forth of the Book of Mormon are amazing, both for their message and, in the case of Nephi's account, their detail. They show us the importance of this book in the grand scheme of things as well as its prominence during the culminating events that will lead up to the Second Coming of the Lord. When I ponder these verses, I come to the conclusion that the Book of Mormon is the central point around which all other events hinge. Because of the Book of Mormon, the events of the last days will transpire without violating the laws and demands of justice and mercy. The children of men will have the chance to prepare for the Lord's return, armed with knowledge and faith, to receive him with joy and gladness. Because of the Book of Mormon, the gospel was restored and The Church of Jesus Christ was once more established on the earth. Once more temples dot the land and the saving ordinances performed therein are bringing the hope of salvation to millions.

Notes

1. Sidney B. Sperry, *Answers to Book of Mormon Questions* (Salt Lake City: Bookcraft, 1967), 53–61.
2. "The Testimony of the Three Witnesses," Book of Mormon.
3. Ibid.

7

ABINADI AND KING NOAH

Having completed our exploration of Biblical scriptures in the books of Nephi, we have to pass through four hundred years of history before we again see Isaiah quoted verbatim in the record. This is not to say, however, that prophets after Nephi did not use Isaiah's teachings or know his works. We must remember that the Book of Mormon is an abridgement of much larger records. We may never know what things Mormon was forced to leave out as he struggled to whittle down the vast amount of records in his keeping to produce one reasonably-sized and manageable record for us today. He said he was not able to include the "hundredth part" (3 Nephi 26:6) in his record, and it is fair to suppose that more teachings of Isaiah were delivered to the people that were of great worth to them but not necessarily as valuable to us in this day. Isaiah taught on many subjects and issues, but it seems that the words that have thus far made it into this record all deal with the coming of the Savior both during his mortal ministry as well as during his millennial reign.

From what we have already seen in Nephi's record, as well as the things we shall hear from the Savior later during his visit to the Nephites, it is apparent that Isaiah's teachings were always applicable and timely throughout the generations of Book of Mormon prophets and were of great worth to every person. If we take into account Moroni's statement about the difficulty in writing on the plates and remember the words in the title page stating that the purpose of this record was to convince the Jew and the Gentile that Jesus is the Christ, it then becomes understandable to accept that he might have limited his recording of Isaiah texts to just those messianic prophecies uttered by Book of Mormon prophets.

We are now in the book of Mosiah, and we find the prophet Abinadi in the land of Lehi-Nephi. He has been brought in chains before the wicked King Noah, who was the son of King Zeniff. Noah did not follow in his father's righteous ways but spent his time and his life living riotously and wickedly. He surrounded himself with corrupt priests who joined him in his revelry.

During this appearance before King Noah, these wicked priests asked Abinadi to interpret a passage from Isaiah 52 (Mosiah 12:20, referring to Isaiah 52:7–10). They declared to Abinadi that they had been teaching from Isaiah, yet they did not understand his words. Abinadi's response in Mosiah 12 bears reading.

> 25 And now Abinadi said unto them: Are you priests, and pretend to teach this people, and to understand the spirit of prophesying, and yet desire to know of me what these things mean?
>
> 26 I say unto you, wo be unto you for perverting the ways of the Lord! For if ye understand these things ye have not taught them; therefore, ye have perverted the ways of the Lord.
>
> 27 Ye have not applied your hearts to understanding; therefore, ye have not been wise. Therefore, what teach ye this people?

From this passage it is obvious that Isaiah's words were taught by all the priests and teachers of the day. Even unrighteous priests struggled with and attempted to teach Isaiah to the people.

The priests declared to Abinadi that they had been teaching the law of Moses, but he challenged them again, saying, "If you teach the law of Moses why do you not keep it?" He continued by teaching them the Ten Commandments and revealing the destruction and woe that was about to come upon them because of their wickedness. As this event progresses, things go very badly for Abinadi, and he is about to be put to death for his teachings. As the priests approach to take him away and slay him, he stops them with the following declaration:

> Touch me not, for God shall smite you if ye lay your hands upon me, for I have not delivered the message which the Lord sent me to deliver; neither have I told you that which ye requested that I should tell; therefore, God will not suffer that I shall be destroyed at this time. (Mosiah 13:3)

As he spoke these words, the record says that Abinadi's face shone like

Moses's had on Mount Sinai. (Exodus 34:29). Neither the king's priests nor any of the assembled people dared to touch him for the fear that had come over them. Abinadi was left to deliver the message that he had been commanded to teach. This is significant because the words that Abinadi was commanded to deliver were words from Isaiah! In other words, the Lord had sent him into harm's way and almost certain death to deliver more of Isaiah's messianic teachings. So important was the message that Abinadi was asked to deliver that the Lord had to protect him with heavenly powers to allow him to speak them. With this protection Abinadi was able to clarify some elements of the law of Moses and then deliver the messianic message of Isaiah 53.

Before we take a look at Abinadi's Isaiah 53, we should try to understand why his mission was so important that he should give his life for it. To do this we need to understand some basic tendencies of the people that had been displayed by almost every generation since Moses led the Israelites out of Egypt.

Law of Moses

It had always been a great struggle for the children of Israel to comprehend the concept of a Messiah who would come down to atone for their sins and lead them in righteousness. The first Israelites, in the custody of Pharaoh, knew almost nothing of God and had as their only example Pharaoh, who was a man with seemingly unlimited power. They were jealous and wanted a Hebrew god patterned after him. Pharaoh surrounded himself with idols and graven images, and so the children of Israel wanted the same.

As Moses led them out of bondage and into the desert, Jehovah, through Moses, endeavored to teach them the nature and desire of the one true God who would protect them and always be their strength. But the children of Israel had difficulty dropping their expectations for a strong and powerful tangible god whom they could see, hear, and bow down to. As Moses taught them from the flanks of Mt. Sinai and began putting them under the Lord's covenant, they rebelled and hardened their hearts. They desired a golden calf that they could see and feel and touch over the statutes of an invisible Lord and his servant, Moses. This is referred to in the scriptures as the "first provocation" (Hebrews 3:8), and Alma referred to it when he contended with Zeezrom.

> And now my brethren, behold I say unto you, that if ye will harden your hearts ye shall not enter into the rest of the Lord; therefore your iniquity provoketh him that sendeth down his wrath upon you **as in the first provocation**, yea, according to his word in the last provocation as well as the first, to the everlasting destruction of your souls; therefore, according to his word, unto the last death, as well as the first. (Alma 12:36)

In Doctrine and Covenants 84 we find what this first provocation was.

> Now this Moses plainly taught to the children of Israel in the wilderness, and sought diligently to sanctify his people that they might behold the face of God;
>
> But they hardened their hearts and could not endure his presence; therefore, the Lord in his wrath, for his anger was kindled against them, swore that they should not enter into his rest while in the wilderness, which rest is the fulness of his glory. (vv. 23–24)

The consequence of this hardening of the heart and first provocation is revealed in the next verse.

> Therefore, he took Moses out of their midst, and the Holy Priesthood also. (D&C 84:25)

Because of the people's inability to grasp the simple concept of a great and loving God, who would send his son to make a sacrifice for them, they had suffered in ignorance and confusion about their relationship with him. As a result they repeatedly fell victim to hardening their hearts and esteeming the words of the prophets as of little value. The result of this characteristic was that they seldom enjoyed the blessings and benefits of the Melchizedek Priesthood and its attendant blessings of salvation and sanctification. Instead, they tended to fall back onto the much simpler statutory prohibitions of the law of Moses, thinking, incorrectly, that it would bring them salvation in the next life. They never understood that the whole purpose of the law of Moses was to acquaint them with and teach them about their coming Messiah. For this reason Abinadi could rightly say to them,

> Ye have not applied your hearts to understanding; therefore, ye have not been wise. Therefore, what teach ye these people? (Mosiah 12:27)

All the prophets had been unanimous in their exhortations and revelations about the Savior. They repeatedly stressed that the law of Moses could not save anyone. Its purpose was to teach about the Savior and cause people to believe in him. Once that was accomplished, the law of Moses had no more value. It did not have the saving ordinances of the temple nor did it contain the exalted doctrines of the Melchizedek Priesthood.   This is what Nephi meant when he wrote:

> For, for this end was the law given; wherefore the law hath become dead unto us, and we are made alive in Christ, until the law shall be fulfilled. (2 Nephi 25:25)

As Abinadi stood before King Noah, he tried to put the law of Moses into the proper perspective for them. He states the following in Mosiah 13:

> 29 And now I say unto you that it was expedient that there should be a law given to the children of Israel, yea, even a very strict law; for they were a stiffnecked people, quick to do iniquity, and slow to remember the Lord their God;
> 30 Therefore there was a law given them, yea, a law of performances and ordinances, a law which they were to observe strictly from day to day, to keep them in remembrance of God and their duty towards him.
> 31 But behold, I say unto you, that all these things were types of things to come.
> 32 And now, did they understand the law? I say unto you, Nay, they did not all understand the law; and this because of the hardness of their hearts; for they understood not that there could not any man be saved except it were through the redemption of God.

Abinadi was sent to the land of Lehi-Nephi specifically to deliver the message that there was a Savior and that he would come down to make the atoning sacrifice for them. In the last few verses of Mosiah 13 Abinadi tells them that all the prophets carried this same message to their people. As support for his argument, he calls upon the words of Isaiah.

> 33 For behold, did not Moses prophesy unto them concerning the coming of the Messiah, and that God should redeem his people? Yea, and even all the prophets who have prophesied ever since the world began—have they not spoken more or less concerning these things?
> 34 Have they not said that God himself should come down among the children of men, and take upon him the form of man, and go forth

in mighty power upon the face of the earth?

35 Yea, and have they not said also that he should bring to pass the resurrection of the dead, and that he, himself, should be oppressed and afflicted?

And finally, Abinadi starts his quote of Isaiah 53 by saying, "Yea, even doth not Isaiah say."

At this point Abinadi begins his quotation of Isaiah. He does so to show the assembled priests and King Noah that even the ancient prophet, from whose words they had been teaching, spoke about the Savior and his ultimate sacrifice. The strength of this passage is in the fact that they had been teaching their people from the words of Isaiah long before Abinadi ever showed up in the land of Lehi-Nephi. Isaiah's credibility was already well established among them and though they had difficulty understanding his words, they accepted him as a true prophet. It was, therefore, a natural thing for Abinadi to use the words of one who they already considered a prophet in order to show them the truth of his own admonitions concerning the Savior. His reasoning was that even if they did not all esteem him as a prophet, they would still be reminded of and forced to accept the words of Isaiah.

This was not unlike what Nephi did early on, before the split between the Nephites and the Lamanites, wherein he called upon Isaiah to support the things he was trying to teach the people. Like Abinadi, Nephi was addressing people, not all of who accepted him as a true prophet, but who did accept Isaiah.

Isaiah 53

With the exception of one word, the Book of Mormon transcript of Isaiah 53 is identical to that found in the Bible. The one difference is found in Mosiah 14:9. The biblical passage uses the word *violence* in lieu of the word *evil* as found in Mosiah.

This chapter of Isaiah is one of the more easily understood passages of all his writings. It takes no real stretch to follow the clear and accurate description of the Savior and what he endured during his mortal ministry. However, there are some interesting things to be found in this passage, so let's take it a few verses at a time.

1 Yea, even doth not Isaiah say: Who hath believed our report, and to whom is the arm of the Lord revealed?

2 For he shall grow up before him as a tender plant, and as a root out of dry ground; he hath no form nor comeliness; and when we shall see him there is no beauty that we should desire him.

3 He is despised and rejected of men; a man of sorrows, and acquainted with grief; and we hid as it were our faces from him; he was despised, and we esteemed him not.

Isaiah pretty well describes the life of the Savior in two verses. The imagery of a tender plant in verse 2 refers to his purity and unspoiled nature. The root out of dry ground shows that he brings life out of a life-less environment. Roots were a very common and popular image in the days of Isaiah. Being an agrarian society, all the people understood the importance of having good ground in which to grow their crops. They all understood that for a good yield of their crops, they needed to till and cultivate the soil. They needed rich soil full of nutrients, and they needed water to make the plants grow. Isaiah's use of the term "as a root out of dry ground" was a statement that this pure oracle of truth would spring forth from a place thirsting and wasting away in ignorance. He was saying that Jesus was not a product of a spiritually fertile and vibrant society. He did not come because the times and the society fostered such growth. He sprang forth out of dry ground.

Verse 2 also makes the statement, often quoted, that "there is no beauty that we should desire him." This does not necessarily mean that Jesus was not an attractive or handsome man. Rather, it should be taken to indicate that Jesus's credibility was not based on his physical prowess or desirability. In our day and time we give extraordinary honor and glory to people based on their looks, power, and wealth. Millions of people idolize movie stars solely because they are beautiful or handsome. Fans adore our most popular public figures often without knowing anything about their personal habits, values, or integrity. We don't seem to care when they get arrested for bad behavior or ethics. It seems some people even adore them all the more when they are "bad boys" or "bad girls."

Isaiah was making the point that Jesus was not (apologies to Andrew Lloyd Weber) a superstar. He was born the mortal son of a carpenter and his very special wife, Mary.

Verse 3 states quite clearly how most of the world esteemed the Savior. Isaiah's primary message was, however, that Jesus would have to do his mission on his own. He would not have the popular support of the public. Isaiah says we "hid our faces from him . . . and we esteemed him not."

105

The Savior's mission was a solitary mission. Certainly, he had disciples who followed him and transmitted his message throughout the land, but the real mission of the Savior—the Atonement and ultimately his sacrifice—was his alone to accomplish.

With verses 4–8, Isaiah tells, as plainly as a prophet could foresee, the trials and tribulations of the Savior associated with the actual Atonement as he experienced it in Gethsemane and upon the cross at Calvary.

> 4 Surely he has borne our griefs, and carried our sorrows; yet we did esteem him stricken, smitten of God, and afflicted.
>
> 5 But he was wounded for our transgressions, he was bruised for our iniquities; the chastisement of our peace was upon him; and with his stripes we are healed.
>
> 6 All we, like sheep, have gone astray; we have turned every one to his own way; and the Lord hath laid on him the iniquities of us all.
>
> 7 He was oppressed, and he was afflicted, yet he opened not his mouth; he is brought as a lamb to the slaughter, and as a sheep before her shearers is dumb so he opened not his mouth.
>
> 8 He was taken from prison and from judgment; and who shall declare his generation? For he was cut off out of the land of the living; for the transgressions of my people he was stricken.

In these five short verses Isaiah tells the story of the Atonement and Crucifixion of the Savior. Verse 4 takes place in the garden where the Lord made his great intercessory prayer. It was a prayer like no other ever uttered—during the course of it, the Lord was stricken with the burdens, sorrows, fears, and guilt of every sin ever committed by people since the earth began. His was no intellectual or compassionate pondering of the human condition; rather, he was made to feel the actual pains that accompany the guilt of sin. He physically experienced the agony of despair that leads some people to commit transgression. He felt the debilitating effects of depression and desperation that lead others to sacrifice their integrity. He also felt and understood the hatred that rages in the souls of so many men and felt what they felt when they acted out their anger upon the helpless and the weak of the world.

He likewise comprehended the intoxication of power that leads corrupt men to reign with terror upon the earth to satisfy their own lust and greed. In fine, the Lord, during that agonizing prayer in Gethsemane, truly felt everything that humans can and have ever felt. He experienced the motivations that lead us to sin and gained the first-hand understanding not only of what humans are capable of committing but also of why they commit such sins. So complete was the Savior's experience in Gethsemane that not one of us will be able to say at the judgment day, "You don't know what it was like." The Savior will tell us as he told Joseph Smith in Liberty Jail, "If the very jaws of hell shall gape open the mouth wide after thee, know thou, my son, that all these things shall give thee experience, and shall be for thy good. The Son of Man hath descended below them all. Art thou greater than he?" (D&C 122:7–8).

Verse 5 tells us that the Savior was a victim throughout this process. He was wounded and bruised and made to suffer chastisement and the lashes of the scourge[1] for us. Verse 6 indicts us all, stating that every one of us has gone astray. The Savior's Atonement was universal. He was made to suffer for the sins committed by every person who ever lived, whether they ultimately come to accept him or not. What a waste it will be for those who fail to take advantage of the great sacrifice made by the Lord on their behalf.

Verses 7 and 8 relate the experience of the Savior as he appeared before Pilate, at his trial, and before his actual death upon the cross. He suffered the events of his last day silently and humbly. He spoke only a few words during his actual crucifixion, giving charge to John concerning Mary and declaring from the cross that it was over.

The Savior's plaintive plea from the cross—wherein he cried out, "My God, my God, why hast thou forsaken me?"—has caused much debate among scholars and followers. It seems the world has misunderstood this utterance and taken it as a sign of last minute weakness or a trial of faith. This is incorrect. For the Atonement to be complete, the Savior had to suffer and experience the absolute worst that man could suffer. As was just quoted from Doctrine and Covenants 122, the Savior declared that he had "descended below them all."

Of all the things that man can suffer, surely the fate of those who become "sons of perdition" is the worst. We are told that even the telestial kingdom, the kingdom known to the world as hell, is a kingdom of glory (D&C 76:89). In perdition, however, there is no glory. It is called outer darkness because there is a complete and utter withdrawal of the Spirit. It is a place of hopelessness and despair. It holds no promise of ultimate redemption or salvation. The emotional suffering and anguish of one consigned to that place can only be guessed, yet we know for that brief moment during which the Savior felt the complete withdrawal of the Spirit, he was caused to cry out in despair, "Why hast thou forsaken me?" (Matthew 27:46). That experience was so horrifyingly awful that it could not be experienced in the garden and was saved until the very last moment on the cross.

As soon as he had suffered that portion of the Atonement, the Lord knew he had seen every condition that man could encounter and was thus able to declare, "Father, into thy hands I commend my spirit" (Luke 23:46).

The Atonement and the Crucifixion

Verses 10 and 11 are Isaiah's explanation of why the Savior endured the Atonement and Crucifixion. In verse 10 Isaiah starts by saying, "Yet it pleased the Lord to bruise him." Let's look at the whole verse and figure out why he said that.

> 10 Yet it pleased the Lord to bruise him; he hath put him to grief; when thou shalt make his soul an offering for sin he shall see his seed, he shall prolong his days, and the pleasure of the Lord shall prosper in his hand.

As we scrutinize this verse we must keep in mind that Old Testament prophets did not make a clear distinction between Jehovah or Jesus, and Elohim (our Heavenly Father). The prophets used the term *Lord* to represent the greater Godhead and trusted in the truth that whether the Father or the Son says it, it is the same. This also gets back to that issue we encountered in Nephi regarding the "manner of speaking of the Jews."

So, verse 10 essentially says, "It pleased Heavenly Father to bruise the Savior." Of course we know that Heavenly Father loves the Savior as his Only Begotten Son. It would be foolish to think that he actually enjoyed seeing his son suffer. Rather, Isaiah was saying that it was a joyous thing the Savior was accomplishing by submitting himself to the pains and agony of the Atonement. He was unlocking salvation and exaltation for all those who would follow him. He was bringing to pass the pivotal event in all of human history. Had the Atonement not been made, this whole earth, and all the inhabitants therein would have been wasted. Billions of spirits would have been lost for the eternities, unable to fulfill the purpose of their creation, unable to continue on to become like their heavenly parents. Their eternal progression would have been stopped, and they truly would have been damned. It was certainly pleasing to Heavenly Father, as well as to all the heavenly hosts who witnessed it, to see Christ fulfill his duty as our Savior and unlock the keys to heaven and let us in.

Verse 10 also says, "When thou shalt make his soul an offering for sin he shall see his seed." This is a statement by Isaiah to us as humans. He states that when we recognize the Savior's sacrifice, when we develop sufficient faith in him that we rely on that sacrifice to pay for our sins, we shall then become his sons and his daughters. We shall become his seed. We do this by baptism, wherein we take upon ourselves the name of the Son just as we take upon ourselves the name of our parents when we are born into our individual families. One becomes a Smith, another a Jones, another a Gomez, and so on throughout the world. We all become members of the family of Christ when we are baptized in his name. This is the new birth, or being born again, as referred to in the scriptures (see John 3:7). This is how the Savior can say, " I am the Father and the Son." In Ether we read:

> Behold, I am he who was prepared from the foundation of the world to redeem my people. Behold, I am Jesus Christ. I am the Father and the Son. In me shall all mankind have life, and that eternally, even they who shall become my sons and my daughters. (Ether 3:14)

Thus, Isaiah was correct in saying that when we accept Jesus' sacrifice, he will then be able to look upon his seed.

Verse 11 tells how the Atonement works and it is best explained by the Doctrine and Covenants. Let's look at the verse in Mosiah first.

> He shall see the travail of his soul and shall be satisfied; by his knowledge shall my righteous servant justify many; for he shall bear their iniquities. (Mosiah 14:11)

In 1831 the prophet Joseph received a revelation, now recorded as Doctrine and Covenants 45, in which the nature of the Savior's relationship to us was further explained. In it the Lord explains his role as our advocate, or lawyer, who stands before God pleading our case. His defense of us is based upon our faith in him, and he makes that case because of the sacrifice he made and the right it granted him to plead for us. He says:

> Listen to him who is the advocate with the Father, who is pleading your cause before him—
> Saying: Father, behold the suffering and death of him who did

no sin, in whom thou wast well pleased; behold the blood of thy Son which was shed, the blood of him whom thou gavest that thyself might be glorified;

Wherefore, Father, spare these my brethren that believe on my name, that they may come unto me and have everlasting life. (vv. 3–5)

Because of the Savior's pleading, Isaiah says Heavenly Father "shall see the travail of his soul and shall be satisfied." No other soul in creation will have the power or have earned the right to stand before the Father and make such a claim as will the Savior.

This chapter of Isaiah could end right here except for that "manner of speaking of the Jews" that keeps cropping up. It was the nature of Jewish speaking that required a recapitulation, or "restatement" of the message at the end. Isaiah signs off this chapter by repeating and summarizing the things he has just said. He states:

12 Therefore will I divide him a portion with the great, and he shall divide the spoil with the strong; because he hath poured his soul out unto death; and he was numbered with the transgressors; and he bore the sins of many, and made intercession for the transgressors.

In other words, we will be made joint-heirs with Christ in all the Father has because of the burdens he took upon himself at Gethsemane and Golgotha.

This was the message Abinadi was sent to deliver to King Noah. It was not a message of condemnation, but rather a message of hope. It gave the king, and any who listened, the chance to repent and come to Jesus. It told the king that the Savior would bear the burden of his wicked ways and would intercede on his behalf. Noah could yet turn from wickedness and enjoy the eternal salvation of his forefathers. It was a powerful message, and it had great effect upon the king. As Abinadi pled his case before the king over the next few days, the record says he caused fear in Noah's heart.

And now king Noah was about to release him, for he feared his word; for he feared that the judgments of God would come upon him. (Mosiah 17:11)

In the end, though, the wicked priests prevailed on the king to condemn Abinadi to death. Abinadi's own prophetic words guaranteed that Noah would suffer the same death that he administered to Abinadi, yet it was not by way of curse but rather, a consequence of Noah's own decisions and actions.

Trust in the Lord

When we consider this story, and Abinadi's inclusion of Isaiah's text in it, we must stand back and take in the broader lesson of the scriptures as presented. Remember, Abinadi stopped the priests from taking him and executing him by stating that they could have no power over him for a while because he had "not delivered the message which the Lord sent [him] to deliver" (Mosiah 13:3). The Lord sent Abinadi to Noah to deliver a message of repentance and faith. The text from Isaiah 53 is a message of hope and a call to put trust in the Lord. It is a clear and lucid explanation of the Savior's birth, life, ministry, and death. The message delivered to King Noah was that if he would put his faith in the Lord he would be saved. This is astounding because we, as mere mortals, would look upon King Noah's life as the very representation of idolatry and evil. He had apparently repudiated everything that his forbearers had believed in. We would probably have expected the Lord to send Abinadi to Noah simply to pronounce condemnation and woe, yet the message delivered was one of hope and possibility.

Even a man such as Noah had the potential to be saved if he would humble himself and repent. The lesson here is that it is not too late to repent. It's never too late to repent. Had Noah repented he could have eventually found favor with the Lord. The apparent curse that Abinadi pronounced upon King Noah was really nothing more than a promise that Noah would suffer the same fate as he chose to impose upon Abinadi. It was not God who would curse King Noah but rather Noah himself who would suffer the consequences of his own actions. Abinadi did not go to the land of Lehi-Nephi to condemn King Noah. He was sent there to try to change him and call him to repentance. He was commanded by the Lord to deliver the words of Isaiah 53 so that King Noah would understand who this Jesus Christ was, that he had heard so much about as a child. He was sent to tell the wicked king that it is never too late to repent and the king could, if he chose, still be favored of the Lord.

This idea of sending messengers to wicked kings is not unique to Abinadi and King Noah. In Alma we read about Ammon and his travels to the land of Ishmael where he encountered King Lamoni. In Alma 17 we read about the nature of these people:

> And assuredly it was great, for they had undertaken to preach the word of God to a wild and a ferocious people; a people who delighted in murdering the Nephites, and robbing and plundering them; and their hearts were set upon riches, or upon gold and silver, and precious stones; yet they sought to obtain these things by murdering and plundering, that they might not labor for them with their own hands. (v. 14)

And again we read:

> And as Ammon entered the land of Ishmael, the Lamanites took him and bound him, as was their custom to bind all Nephites who fell into their hands, and carry them before their king; and thus it was left to the pleasure of the king to slay them, or to retain them in captivity, or to cast them into prison, or to cast them out of his land, according to his will and pleasure. (v. 20)

To this point the experience of Ammon was not so different from that of Abinadi just sixty years earlier. Yet he was able to touch the king's heart and effect a great change in him. Indeed, so great was his change that he fell into a trance as if dead, only to awaken as a changed man with a testimony. As soon as he was awake he began preaching to his people and converted many.

> And when she [Lamoni's wife] had said this, she clasped her hands, being filled with joy, speaking many words which were not understood; and when she had done this, she took the king, Lamoni, by the hand, and behold he arose and stood upon his feet.
>
> And he, immediately, seeing the contention among his people, went forth and began to rebuke them, and to teach them the words which he had heard from the mouth of Ammon; and as many as heard his words believed, and were converted. (Alma 19:30–31)

Alma finishes this account of King Lamoni with the following observation:

> And it came to pass that there were many that did believe in their words; and as many as did believe were baptized; and they became a righteous people, and they did establish a church among them.
>
> And thus, the work of the Lord did commence among the Lamanites; thus the Lord did pour out his Spirit upon them; and we see that his arm is extended to all people who will repent and believe on his name. (Alma 19:35–36)

In the account of Ammon and King Lamoni we see the good that could have occurred for King Noah and his people if he had been converted like King Lamoni.

The great message of Isaiah 53 is that we can never declare that it is too late for us. The Lord holds out his arm to all who will take hold, and some will take hold. Alma the Younger, the sons of Mosiah, and, in the Bible, the Apostle Paul are all examples of bad men humbling themselves, changing, and going forth in faith to do great and marvelous works.

Though Abinadi was unsuccessful in swaying King Noah's behavior, his words were powerful and delivered by the Spirit. And one among the assembled throng listened, heard, and was moved by the Spirit to repent, and we are the richer for it. It was one of King Noah's priests who began, privately, to teach the people Abinadi's words. Those who heard him and believed fled into the wilderness where the priest established a church and began his long and most productive work for the Lord. We have come to know and love this priest called Alma.

Notes

1. A scourge is a whip with bits of bone or metal shards embedded into the tips of the leather. As the victim was lashed, the bone and metal would rip gashes in the flesh. Oftentimes, the scourge would remove strips of flesh from the victim.

8

THE SAVIOR'S VISIT TO THE AMERICAS

We have now come to the advent of the Savior's visit to the American continents less than a year after his crucifixion and resurrection. The exact amount of time that had elapsed since his resurrection is not certain but scholars agree that it was not during the Pentecost,[1] and that sufficient time had passed for the inhabitants of Mesoamerica to have reassembled after the destructions that befell the New World. Some reconstruction had begun and people were trying to make sense of the great changes that had occurred.

The Savior's visit fulfilled the prophecy of Samuel the Lamanite concerning his appearance to the Nephites and Lamanites who would survive the destruction. His time in the New World was marked by many great miracles and healings of the sick and the infirm. Marvelous teachings were put forth, and they were of such a great and sacred nature that Mormon records the words of Nephi as saying:

> And no tongue can speak, neither can there be written by any man, neither can the hearts of men conceive so great things as we both saw and heard Jesus speak; and no one can conceive of the joy which filled our souls at the time we heard him pray for us unto the Father. (3 Nephi 17:17)

The record states that this was a time of great teaching and that even the mouths of the little children were opened. Their tongues were loosed that they uttered great and marvelous things such as had never been heard before. Mormon says:

> Therefore I would that ye should behold that the Lord truly did teach the people, for the space of three days; and after that he did show himself unto them oft, and did break bread oft, and bless it, and give it unto them.
>
> And it came to pass that he did teach and minister unto the children of the multitude of whom hath been spoken, and he did loose their tongues, and they did speak unto their fathers great and marvelous things, even greater than he had revealed unto the people; and he loosed their tongues that they could utter. (3 Nephi 26:13–14)

During this time the Lord expounded upon the scriptures that the people had with them. He also reviewed the records that had been kept by the Nephites and edited them. In one instance the Lord found an omission in Nephi's record and commanded that it be fixed.

> And it came to pass that he said unto Nephi: Bring forth the records which ye have kept.
>
> And when Nephi had brought forth the records, and laid them before him, he cast his eyes upon them and said:
>
> Verily I say unto you, I commanded my servant Samuel, the Lamanite, that he should testify unto this people, that at the day that the Father should glorify his name in me that there were many saints who should arise from the dead, and should appear unto many, and should minister unto them. And he said unto them: Was it not so?
>
> And his disciples answered him and said: Yea, Lord, Samuel did prophesy according to thy words, and they were all fulfilled.
>
> And Jesus said unto them: How be it that ye have not written this thing, that many saints did arise and appear unto many and did minister unto them?
>
> And it came to pass that Nephi remembered that this thing had not been written.
>
> And it came to pass that Jesus commanded that it should be written; therefore it was written according as he commanded. (3 Nephi 23:7–13)

During the course of the Savior's visit we find three separate passages of Biblical scriptures included in his teachings. These include a new, first person delivery of a text we find in the Gospel of Matthew known as the Sermon on the Mount. The New World version of the Sermon on the Mount was delivered almost immediately upon the Savior's arrival and, though it is not a verbatim copy of his sermon delivered in Jerusalem, it was essentially the same message. Being that it was delivered by the same person, and seeing that it contains the same message, it merits consideration in this work as a biblical reference. In this way it is somewhat like Nephi's version of Isaiah 29 that we studied in chapter 6. It is the same text as the biblical account, redelivered with appropriate changes to fit the circumstances.

The next set of scriptures spoken by the Savior is the text from Isaiah 54, included in a sermon he delivered to the assembled throng, during which he made numerous quotes of other, individual scriptures as well. While his talk drew upon various sources, he took the time to quote Isaiah 54 in its entirety, though not from the Nephite record specifically. Having been the author of the same words to Isaiah, it is understandable that the Lord could quote them to the Nephites.

It was of great importance to the Lord that the Nephite records be accurate and complete. He also placed great value on the more ancient records, which the people had brought with them from Jerusalem. He reviewed what records they possessed and, after completing his audit, determined that there were other records they needed. Mormon records the following:

> And now it came to pass that when Jesus had said these words he
> said unto them again, after he had expounded all the scriptures unto
> them which they had received, he said unto them: Behold, other scrip-
> tures I would that ye should write, that ye have not. (3 Nephi 26:3)

These other scriptures are the words of Malachi, which the Savior delivered to the Nephites. These were records the Nephites did not have with them because they had left Jerusalem before the words were spoken by Malachi. Jesus spoke the words almost verbatim from the account we find in the King James Version of the Bible. He made this comment after he had expounded upon them:

> And he saith: These scriptures, which ye had not with you, the
> Father commanded that I should give unto you; for it is wisdom in him
> that they should be given for future generations. (3 Nephi 26:2)

So, in the book of 3 Nephi, we have biblical scriptures (Isaiah) that the Nephites already had with them, new scriptures spoken after they left Jerusalem and given to them directly by the Savior (Malachi), and finally the Sermon on the Mount, delivered fresh from the Savior's mouth to the

Nephites, adapted to their time and place but consistent enough with the gospel of Matthew that it can be considered Biblical text.

Isaiah 54

Though the Savior delivered the modified version of the Sermon on the Mount prior to his quotes of Isaiah or Malachi, we will examine the Isaiah text first so that we may complete our study of Isaiah as found in the Book of Mormon. This will complete our examination of biblical texts from sources that were in the possession of the Nephites from the time they left Jerusalem. Once that is complete, we will take a look at the new text from Malachi that the Savior added to their records. Finally, we will study the Lord's "Sermon on the Mount" as delivered to the Nephites and Lamanites.

This chapter from Isaiah completes a set, which runs from Isaiah 48 to 54. Chapters 48 and 49 were found in 1 Nephi; chapters 50, 51, and part of 52 were found in 2 Nephi; chapter 53, delivered to King Noah by Abinadi; and now, in 3 Nephi 22, we read the Lord's presentation of Isaiah 54.

Reading in 3 Nephi 20, we see that the Lord first administered the sacrament, after which he began a sermon concerning the mission, future, and destiny of the house of Israel. He prefaced his words with this introduction:

> 11 Ye remember that I spake unto you, and said that when the words of Isaiah should be fulfilled—behold they are written, ye have them before you, therefore search them—
> 12 And verily, verily, I say unto you, that when they shall be fulfilled then is the fulfilling of the covenant which the Father hath made unto his people, O house of Israel.

It is interesting that the Savior himself, as an introduction to his own teaching, should reference Isaiah. It certainly makes Isaiah an unimpeachable source of knowledge for one seeking to understand the will of the Father. The Savior's reminder that the people possessed the words of Isaiah and that they should search them should be considered a commandment to us all. Indeed, the Savior will have more to say about that very thing in a few more chapters.

As Jesus spoke, he quoted and referenced many verses from throughout the Old Testament. His teachings covered things said in all the books of the Pentateuch[2] as well as the prophecies of later prophets. He spoke primarily about the destiny of Israel. He also spoke concerning the ultimate gathering and reestablishment of the house of Israel and promised that Israel would assume its proper place among all the people of the world. By referencing Israel, he was not speaking particularly about the nation we now know as Israel but rather about the kingdom of God as administered by the house of Israel, who possessed the right to the priesthood because of the covenant of Abraham. This would include all the scattered people throughout the world who will ultimately gather back and come into the knowledge of their heritage and the covenants of the Father, that were made to them. He wanted the Nephites and Lamanites to know of their contribution to this restoration, through the Book of Mormon. He wanted them to understand that bigger things, more than just their mortal existences, were being put into motion and that they had a part in that. His message was a message of hope and comfort. Isaiah 54 speaks to these very things, so it was very appropriate that the Lord should take the time to remind them of these things and explain Isaiah's words to them.

The Lord's rendering of Isaiah 54 is found in 3 Nephi 22. It begins by issuing a proclamation of hope and rejoicing, for the house of Israel will be gathered back again and those who have not been able to rejoice before will finally be able to. The first three verses speak to this:

> 1 And then shall that which is written come to pass: Sing, O barren, thou that didst not bare; break forth into singing, and cry aloud, thou that didst not travail with child; for more are the children of the desolate than the children of the married wife, saith the Lord.
>
> 2 Enlarge the place of thy tent, and let them stretch forth the curtains of thy habitations; spare not, lengthen thy cords and strengthen thy stakes;
>
> 3 For thou shalt break forth on the right hand and on the left, and thy seed shall inherit the Gentiles and make desolate the cities of the inhabited.

In Isaiah 49, Isaiah spoke to the desolate, as referred to in verse 1, when he said, speaking for Israel: "I have lost my children, and am desolate, a captive, removing to and fro" (Isaiah 49:21), meaning that the perpetuation of the house of Israel as a powerful kingdom would cease. Here, he is saying that they will see the establishment of their families within the kingdom of the Lord. He speaks to the vast numbers of people who will return, saying their numbers are greater than the numbers of the people who are already joined to the kingdom. Verse 2 continues to make this point. Verse 3 states that they shall inherit the Gentiles, which sounds a bit odd. Throughout Old Testament times the Israelites were continually commanded to remove themselves from the Gentiles and to not be influenced by their pagan ways. To understand this promise, that they will inherit the Gentiles, we need to look at the promises of the Abrahamic covenant.

Abraham was promised that any and all who would accept the gospel would be adopted into his house and would be counted as his seed (Abraham 2:10). This was the great promise that made it possible to say that his seed would be as numberless as the sands of the sea. Here, in verse 3, is an iteration of that promise and the statement of when it would be fulfilled. This shall be the day that those Gentiles who accept the gospel will be counted as members of the house of Israel and become part of the covenant people, sharing in the blessings of Abraham.

Verse 4 refers to the travails and tribulations experienced by the Israelites throughout history. Theirs has been a sad tale of hatred, persecution, and death at the hands of any and all who dealt with them. Even today, most Arab nations refuse to even acknowledge Israel's very right to exist. In verses 5 and 6 the Lord promises that this will not always be so:

> 4 Fear not, for thou shalt not be ashamed; neither be thou confounded, for thou shalt not be put to shame; for thou shalt forget the shame of thy youth, and shall not remember the reproach of thy youth, and shalt not remember the reproach of thy widowhood any more.
>
> 5 For thy maker, thy husband, the Lord of Hosts is his name; and thy Redeemer, the Holy One of Israel—God of the whole earth shall he be called.
>
> 6 For the Lord hath called thee as a woman forsaken and grieved in spirit, and a wife of youth, when thou wast refused, saith thy God.

The use of the term *widowhood* hearkens to the fact that the Savior is often referred to as the groom, and his Church, or his kingdom, as the bride. The Lord considers the Church as his bride and the members of the church as his children. This is verified in the book of Ether wherein the Lord says:

> Behold, I am Jesus Christ. I am the Father and the Son. In me shall all mankind have life, and that eternally, even they who shall

believe on my name; and **they shall become my sons and my daughters**. (Ether 3:14; emphasis added)

When the Jews repudiated the Lord, and had him crucified, they, in effect, divorced themselves from him. The Hebrew faith did not acknowledge him as its "husband" and the people of the faith did not accept him as their Father or Savior. He had become, quite literally, dead to them. They were, in effect, widowed. In verses 5 and 6 the Lord is saying that that will all change and they will accept him. They will rejoice to have him as their Savior and their Father. The Hebrew faith and the House of Israel will once again be married to the Holy One of Israel, whom it will finally recognize as Jesus Christ.

Verses 7 and 8 are very sweet and tender in their spirit of forgiveness for the failures of the house of Israel throughout the ages. The Lord says:

> 7 For a small moment have I forsaken thee, but with great mercies will I gather thee.
> 8 In a little wrath I hid my face from thee for a moment, but with everlasting kindness will I have mercy on thee, saith the Lord thy Redeemer.

Verse 8 is a very interesting verse. It can be cross-referenced directly to Doctrine and Covenants 84, where it says:

> Now this Moses plainly taught to the children of Israel in the wilderness, and sought diligently to sanctify his people that they might behold the face of God.
> But they hardened their hearts and could not endure his presence, therefore the Lord in his wrath, for his anger was kindled against them, swore that they should not enter into his rest while in the wilderness, which rest is the fulness of his glory.
> Therefore, he took Moses out of their midst, and the Holy Priesthood also. (vv. 23–25)

Moses had been trying to endow the people with the knowledge, faith, and righteousness they would need to be able to enter the presence of the Lord. When they refused him and built the golden calf instead, they demonstrated their lack of worthiness before Lord. As we saw earlier, this is referred to in Alma as the "first provocation." This event triggered the actions referred to in Isaiah 54 and 3 Nephi 22.

> 9 For this is as the waters of Noah unto me: for as I have sworn

that the waters of Noah should no more go over the earth; so have I sworn that I would not be wroth with thee, nor rebuke thee.

The Lord here makes the promise that the separation that occurred between him and the house of Israel will never occur again. He uses a strange phraseology by starting the verse with: "For this is as the waters of Noah unto me." When the flood covered the earth and cleansed it of all mankind (save Noah and his family) in order to bring about a new beginning, the Lord, as Jehovah, swore that he would never use that drastic measure again. Here, he is dealing specifically with the house of Israel instead of the whole world. The Lord is saying that he will never separate himself from the house of Israel as he did after their repudiation of him and his law at the base of Mt. Sinai.

There is a paradox with verse 9, as well as with all of the verses we have looked at thus far in this chapter. It is this: these words were first spoken by Isaiah in about 700 BC. At that time Israel had not yet rejected her Lord! The Jews had not yet crucified him, and the reproach, persecution, and hatred we commonly associate with Israel had not yet occurred. Even as the Savior spoke these words to the Nephites at the meridian of time, and almost immediately after having been put to death by these same people, he is speaking of forgiveness. He almost sounds remorseful about the separation that most scholars would say had yet to occur.

Certainly, the events of the next two millennia after the crucifixion show that the house of Israel has not had an easy time of it, and their problems continue to this day. So, how is it that the Lord can be sitting among the Nephites speaking of reconciliation when, as far as most of the world is concerned, the separation has only just occurred?

To understand this matter and find the answer, we need to think more broadly and more eternally. We need to consider that perhaps mere trifling matters of a terrestrial world were of no concern to Isaiah as he prophesied. Perhaps he was speaking in a different manner (the manner of the Jews?) and perhaps he was more concerned about more permanent types of separation. We spoke of the "first provocation" that occurred at the foot of Mt. Sinai. Though the Lord was wroth with Israel because of her rejection of his higher laws, he still endeavored to speak to and guide her through prophets. When the Israelites demanded kings he gave them Saul, then David, and finally Solomon. After that failed he gave them judges. Finally, after the kingdom of Judah had fallen into the servitude of foreign kings, the Lord surreptitiously led them with his prophets such as Jeremiah, Ezekiel, and Isaiah. Angels heralded the Savior's birth, and the Lord called men such as John the Baptist to bear the Levitical priesthood. It is obvious that the Lord, first as Jehovah, and then as Jesus Christ, never faltered in his efforts to nurture his people. So again, just what was this separation, or this widowhood, spoken about by Isaiah?

The answer is this: the house of Israel first rejected the Lord when they rejected the higher laws and covenants of the Melchizedek priesthood as offered to them by Moses at Mt. Sinai. They accepted the covenants associated with the Aaronic or Levitical Priesthood as Moses was instructed to present to them, but when he returned from visiting the Lord for the third time, with the Law of Christ and the Melchizedek covenants in hand, they rejected him outright. Doctrine and Covenants 84:25–26 says:

> Therefore, he took Moses out of their midst, and the Holy Priesthood also.
>
> And the lesser priesthood continued, which priesthood holdeth the keys of the ministering of angels and the preparatory gospel.

The loss of the Melchizedek Priesthood among the "rank and file" of the house of Israel was a huge disappointment to the Lord. Doctrine and Covenants 107 tells us that the higher or Melchizedek Priesthood holds the keys of all the spiritual blessings of the Church, including the privilege of receiving the mysteries of the kingdom of Heaven, having the heavens opened unto them, the right to commune with the general assembly and Church of the Firstborn, and the right to enjoy the communion with and presence of the Father and the Son.

The loss of the Melchizedek Priesthood meant the loss of those same privileges. Moses knew this and Doctrine and Covenants 84:21–22 clearly states:

> And without the ordinances thereof, and the authority of the priesthood, the power of godliness is not manifest unto man in the flesh;
>
> For without this no man can see the face of God, even the Father, and live.

For the house of Israel, the loss of the Melchizedek Priesthood meant they could not take part in any of the ordinances of the temple. There was no sealing in marriage for eternity and no sealing of children to their families. There was no conduit for the ordinances required for entry into the kingdom of the Lord to be obtained. Without these sealing ordinances the people, as the bride, could not be married to their groom (the Lord). In truth, the widowhood of Israel started at the beginning of their history, there in the desert at Mt. Sinai. The imagery, used by Isaiah in his prophecy, of the bride rejected in her youth, was most appropriate.

These verses are all talking about the time to come in which the members of the whole house of Israel will, once and for all, accept the Savior as their Messiah and receive his priesthood with all its saving ordinances and privileges. Since these are eternal principles and covenants, they will never depart once they have been accepted. The Lord says as much in verse 10.

> 10 For the mountains shall depart and the hills be removed, but my kindness shall not depart from thee, neither shall the covenant of my peace be removed, saith the Lord that hath mercy on thee.

The Lord pronounces blessings and prosperity upon the house of Israel in verses 11 and 12, and then in verse 13 speaks of their families.

> 13 And all thy children shall be taught of the Lord; and great shall be the peace of thy children.

After that nice pronouncement verses 14, 15, and 17 address an issue that would certainly be of pressing concern for Israel today. Isaiah says:

> 14 In righteousness shalt thou be established; thou shalt be far from oppression for thou shalt not fear, and from terror for it shall not come near thee.
> 15 Behold, they shall surely gather together against thee, not by me; whosoever shall gather together against thee shall fall for thy sake. . . .
> 17 No weapon that is forged against thee shall prosper; and every tongue that revile against thee in judgment thou shalt condemn. This is the heritage of the servants of the Lord, and their righteousness is of me, saith the Lord.

Today, the promise that Israel could be in a position to not fear terror because it would be far from it would be just about the best news that they could hear. The Lord agrees that terrorists and other enemies will gather, but he guarantees that they will ultimately fail. Israel would claim those blessings today if they could, but verse 14 puts on a condition that must first be met. It says: "In righteousness shalt thou be established." When the Jews, and by extension, the house of Israel, establish themselves in righteousness, or in other words, in the gospel, then shall they be free from all oppressors and terrorists. Then "no weapon that is forged against thee shall prosper."

As the Savior delivered these words to the Nephites they must have been filled with the spirit of love. As ones who had accepted the Lord and were partakers of his blessings through the ordinances and covenants of the Melchizedek Priesthood, they probably had a better understanding of what was being said than did the Jews in Jerusalem at the time of Isaiah.

One last verse in this chapter deserves some attention. The Lord indicates, in verse 16, that the trials and tribulations experienced by the Israelites were not all in vain. He speaks of the tests they went through as the refiner's fire, producing a people that the Lord could use to finish his work. He says:

> 16 Behold, I have created the smith that bloweth the coals in the fire, and that bringeth forth an instrument for his work; and I have created the waster to destroy.

After finishing this part of his sermon, the Savior issued a ringing endorsement for Isaiah and a commandment to the people in 3 Nephi 23.

> And now, Behold, I say unto you, that ye ought to search these things. Yea, a commandment I give unto you that ye search these things diligently; for great are the words of Isaiah.
>
> For surely he spake as touching all things concerning my people which are the house of Israel; therefore it must needs be that he must speak also unto the Gentiles. (vv. 1–2)

It is extraordinary and unique that the Savior should so directly command the people to read a specific collection of texts. Certainly, all the words of all the prophets are of great worth and, in fact, a few verses later he does say: "Search the prophets, for many there be that testify of these things." And yet, it was the words of Isaiah about which the Savior said specifically: "Yea, a commandment I give unto you that ye search these things diligently." We are commanded to read Isaiah. Nephi said that the words of Isaiah were difficult for his people to understand. In fact, he said that no one except those trained in the manner of speaking of the Jews could understand them, yet we are under commandment to read and search them. It is, to say the least, a daunting task but not an impossible one. It is hoped that this exploration of Isaiah in the Book of Mormon has helped you to decipher the prophet's visions and warnings.

We have now finished the Isaiah texts of the Book of Mormon. This also completes the study of the biblical scriptures from the brass plates of Laban that were included in the Book of Mormon. We will now take a look at the additional biblical scriptures given by the Lord directly to the Nephites.

Notes

1. The Pentecost refers to the first fifty days after the Lord's resurrection.
2. The first five books of the Old Testament are commonly called the "Pentateuch." They were all written by Moses.

9

THE WORDS OF MALACHI

Malachi 3

After completing his presentation of Isaiah's writing, and expounding upon all the scriptures he had presented to the Nephites, the Savior asked to see the records kept by Nephi and his predecessors. The Savior then took the occasion to add to their collection with some writings of Malachi. These prophecies and teachings had been spoken by Malachi after Lehi and his people had left Jerusalem. In 3 Nephi 26:2, Jesus explained that it was the will of the Father that he deliver these things unto them.

> And he saith: These scriptures, which ye had not with you, the Father commanded that I should give unto you; for it is wisdom in him that they should be given unto future generations.

The Lord presented the text we find in Malachi 3 and 4. This text in the Book of Mormon is identical with the Biblical text except for the introductory words that Mormon appended to the beginning of the recitation. Those introductory words are very interesting because they show that the same pattern used by the Savior was also used by the first Nephi when reading recorded text from ancient prophets. That is, he spoke the words and then took occasion to explain them. This indicates that the people probably had the same difficulty understanding Malachi as they did with Isaiah. Remember that Nephi said the people had difficulty understanding Isaiah, not because it was Isaiah specifically, but rather, because Isaiah spoke according to the manner of the Jews. That being the case, it would be reasonable to assume that Malachi would be just as difficult to understand.

This habit that Book of Mormon prophets (as well as the Savior himself) have of explaining the scriptures after they have spoken them is unique among all the books of scripture. The Bible contains occasions where older scriptures were quoted by the prophets but they were not followed up with explanations. The prophets assumed that the audience understood the manner of speaking of the older prophets because, after all, they were Jews. Book of Mormon prophets, on the other hand, make a very big point about the fact that their people do not understand the manner of speaking of the Jews. It was therefore necessary to explain the scriptures after presenting them. Thus we see, in the beginning of 3 Nephi 24, Mormon's explanatory note prior to the Savior's delivery of Malachi.

> And it came to pass that he commanded them that they should write the words which the Father had given unto Malachi, which he should tell them. And it came to pass that after they were written he expounded them. And these are the words which he did tell unto them, saying. (v. 1)

The first verse of Malachi 3, as found in 3 Nephi 24, shows how confusing Old Testament writings can be. The text requires some explaining to be clear. It says (continued from above):

> Thus said the Father unto Malachi—Behold, I will send my messenger, and he shall prepare the way before me, and the Lord whom ye seek shall suddenly come to his temple, even the messenger of the covenant, whom ye delight in; behold, he shall come, saith the Lord of Hosts.

In this text the identity of the messenger is uncertain and the existence of the temple is a surprise. Also, the method by which the messenger shall prepare the way is unknown. We have heard before the promise of a messenger being sent to prepare the way. In fact, both the Old and the New Testaments have a messenger. In the Old Testament it was Elijah, who would be the "Elias" or forebearer. In the New Testament, we have John the Baptist who some called Elias (or an Elias, with *Elias* serving as a title). This passage in Malachi is an "apocalyptic" prophecy, meaning one referring to the last days and the Second Coming. This time the messenger is not a person and we must turn to the Doctrine and Covenants to uncover its identity. Doctrine and Covenants 45:9 says:

> And even so I have sent mine everlasting covenant into the world to be a light to the world, and to be a standard for my people, and for the Gentiles to seek to it, and **to be a messenger** before my face to prepare the way before me. (Emphasis added)

Here we have a statement that the everlasting covenant is to be the messenger before the coming of the Lord. Of course we could ask, "What does that mean?" Once again we turn to the Doctrine and Covenants for the answer. In Doctrine and Covenants 20:8–9, we read about Joseph Smith's calling and the tasks the Lord assigned him to perform. It reads,

> And gave him power from on high, by the means which were before prepared, to translate the Book of Mormon;
> Which contains a record of a fallen people, and the fulness of the gospel of Jesus Christ to the Gentiles and the Jews also.

And in Doctrine and Covenants 35:12 we read:

> And there are none that doeth good except those who are ready to receive the fulness of my gospel, **which I have sent forth unto this generation**. (Emphasis added)

The everlasting covenant of the Lord is the fulness of the gospel, which includes the priesthood and the saving ordinances and principles of salvation as found in the temples. The Book of Mormon is the instrument that returned the everlasting covenant and the fulness of the gospel to the earth. It is the messenger that was sent to us in the last days to prepare the way for the Lord's return. Malachi said he would appear suddenly in his temple. There were no temples upon the face of the earth until the gospel was restored and the saints erected and dedicated the Kirtland Temple in 1836. When they did, the heavens were opened and numerous heavenly visitors, including Elijah—whom Malachi mentioned directly in Malachi 4:5—came and were seen by many. All of the preparatory steps necessary for the Lord's return were once again in place with the reestablishment of the gospel and his kingdom upon the earth.

We can only speculate whether or not the Nephites understood that the record of the things they were experiencing at that moment and their actions were integral parts of the fulfillment of this prophecy. However, as the Savior expounded upon these things it is highly probable that he showed them their part in the overall scheme.

Next, Malachi pondered the nature of the day of the Lord's coming and who would most benefit from it. In doing so, he revealed to us his understanding of the Savior's mission.

> 2 But who may abide the day of his coming, and who shall stand when he appeareth? For he is like a refiner's fire, and like the fuller's soap.
>
> 3 And he shall sit as a refiner and purifier of silver; and he shall purify the sons of Levi, and purge them as gold and silver, that they may offer unto the Lord an offering in righteousness.
>
> 4 Then shall the offering of Judah and Jerusalem be pleasant unto the Lord, as in the days of old, and as in former years.

The imagery used, that of a refiner's fire or of the fuller's soap, is a common one in Hebrew writing. The refiner's fire is often viewed with some trepidation because fire is commonly linked to images of damnation and hell. However, as Malachi spoke these words they were neither condemnatory nor judgmental. Rather, they expressed hope and showed the true mission and goal of the Savior's work. Both the refiner and the fuller accomplish similar tasks. The refiner removes impurities from metals, making them pure and more precious. The fuller, likewise, is a cleaner. He was the one who would clean and purify lamb's wool in preparation for the making of garments. He would render the base material white and without blemish. Neither of these men threw away or destroyed vast amounts of their base materials in order to find that small pure part. Rather, they took the whole and made it pure. Their job was not to sort and destroy but to cleanse and purify that which was otherwise impure and of no value.

In similar fashion, the Lord is not coming to destroy all the impure. He is coming to make the impure pure. Verse 3 says he will purify the sons of Levi, not destroy or condemn them. He will come to cleanse the earth of falsehood and wickedness. He will do this by teaching truth with the power of his word and the testimony of the Holy Ghost. Only those who refuse to acknowledge him and his truth will perish and await their turn at a later time. The Savior is not coming to wreak vengeance but to bring healing and love. All who accept him will find themselves in his loving embrace.

Verses 3 and 4 also speak of an offering to be made by the sons of Levi on behalf of Judah and Jerusalem. This is the event that is spoken about in Doctrine and Covenants 13. In that section we find the words spoken by John the Baptist as he ordained Joseph Smith and Oliver Cowdery to the Aaronic Priesthood on the banks of the Susquehanna River on May 15, 1829. He said:

> Upon you my fellow servants, in the name of Messiah I confer upon you the Priesthood of Aaron, which holds the keys of the ministering of angels and the gospel of repentance, and of baptism by immersion for the remission of sins; and this shall never be taken Again from the earth, **until the sons of Levi do offer again an offering unto the Lord in righteousness**. (v. 1; emphasis added)

The sons of Levi were the administrators of the Levitical Priesthood. They were the only ones allowed to possess it and to officiate in the various offerings and sacrifices pertaining to it. When the Savior came to earth for his mortal mission, he fulfilled the requirements of the law of Moses and satisfied the obligations of the Levitical ordinances. With his rejection by the ruling and governing councils of the Church, the authority to officiate in the Levitical ordinances was lost and no Levite priest has had the power to conduct an offering in righteousness since.

Historically, only members of the tribe of Levi held the Levitical Priesthood. The slightly broader Aaronic Priesthood was held only by those Levites who were also direct descendents of Aaron, the brother of Moses. When the Levites missed their opportunity at the meridian of time to embrace the Savior and continue their work for him, they lost his authority to exercise the priesthood. When John the Baptist restored that power on the banks of the Susquehanna in 1829, he had to give it to the first non-Levites ever to hold it. That authority rests with The Church of Jesus Christ of Latter-day Saints to this day, but the Abrahamic Covenant still holds it in reserve for the day when the Levites accept the gospel and come unto Christ. At that time they will be entitled to once again officiate in the Levitical and Aaronic ordinances. Returning to our text we can now look at verses 3 and 4 in a new light.

The Lord will purge, or cleanse, the Levites of the impurity of their ignorance. He will teach them the true gospel and remove the darkness of ignorance that has clouded their hearts for two thousand years. With this new understanding and righteousness, they will embrace the gospel. At that time they will be entitled once more to hold and officiate in the

Aaronic ordinances. Both Malachi and Doctrine and Covenants 13 look forward to that time when the house of Judah and the nation of Israel have come to accept Jesus and serve him.

At various places throughout the scriptures the proclamation has been made that the "first shall be last and the last shall be first" (Matthew 20:16). After the Jews rejected Jesus, the job assigned to the house of Israel fell to the Gentiles who, in these latter days, have taken up the mantle and carried the banner for the Lord. We are under mandate to take this gospel to all the families and all the nations of the earth. In the Lord's own due time the land of Israel will be opened up, and the gospel will flow to them. That time, however, will not be until the last, and their acceptance of the gospel will signal the culmination of the preparations for the Savior's triumphal return and the ushering in of the Millennium. As we consider this, we can begin to see the power contained in these first four verses of Malachi. Is it any wonder then that Jesus would speak these words to the Nephites and desire that they should record them?

In the next verse, we see that once the preceding events take place, righteousness and restitution will take place swiftly. As the power of the Lord's law and judgment sweep the earth, those who do wickedly will see their folly and their shame, and evil will be banished. This is what will usher in the new dispensation and the millennial reign.

Verse six shows the strength of a covenant.

> 6 For I am the Lord, I change not; therefore ye sons of Jacob are not consumed.

Though the house of Jacob has rejected their Savior for so many years, they can still claim the promises of the covenant he made with their father Abraham. They shall not be consumed. They will instead be cleansed and purified by their Savior just as silver and gold are purified by the refiner and wool by the fuller.

The next six verses are the verses commonly associated with tithing. They are a strong indictment of those who refuse to acknowledge the Lord's blessing in their lives and a strong promise for those who do.

> 7 Even from the days of your fathers ye are gone away from mine ordinances, and have not kept them. Return unto me and I will return unto you, saith the Lord of Hosts. But ye say: Wherein shall we return?
>
> 8 Will a man rob God? Yet ye have robbed me. But ye say: wherein have we robbed thee? In tithes and offerings.

9 Ye are cursed with a curse, for ye have robbed me, even this whole nation.

10 Bring ye all the tithes into the storehouse, that there might be meat in my house; and prove me now herewith, saith the Lord of Hosts, if I will not open you the windows of heaven, and pour you out a blessing that there shall not be room enough to receive it.

11 And I will rebuke the devourer for your sakes, and he shall not destroy the fruits of your ground; neither shall your vine cast her fruit before the time in the fields, saith the Lord of Hosts.

12 And all nations shall call you blessed, for ye shall be a delightsome land, saith the Lord of Hosts.

Here we find the promise that any offerings we make to the Lord shall be returned to us many times over. This passage is speaking of the law of tithing or the giving of 10 percent of one's increase to the Lord. It is a practice that was lost among the Jews and, for that matter, among most of the world. Verse 9 states that the people are cursed with a curse because they have not been faithful to this principle. If we look at verse 11, we see just what curse they are under. The Lord does not proactively curse a people. Rather, they remove themselves from his protection from evil. Notice that it is not the Lord who will devour their crops or make their vines cast their fruit early. It is the devourer who will do so. While under the protection of the Lord, the devourer is held at bay. Without his protection the devourer has free reign over them and can wreak whatsoever destruction he may.

We have seen this same principle before in Isaiah as we studied the actions of the Lord concerning his unprofitable vineyard. On that occasion God did not destroy the vineyard; he merely withheld the blessings that were keeping the destroyer at bay. In Malachi, the destruction caused by the devourer would follow because the enemy of the people is stronger then they are. The lesson here is that God does not curse us. He is our protector and is working for our protection. As we are obedient we receive his blessings. If we reject him or if we "move out of his house," he is no longer there to protect us, and we are left to fend for ourselves, at which time the devourer seeks his opportunity to swoop down and wreak havoc on our lives.

Verse 12 comes back to the positive side of things and reminds the people what great blessings are in store for them as they obey the commandments.

These verses have a deeper message; one that goes beyond the payment of tithing. Verse 8 says tithes and offerings. Well, tithing is tithing, so what does he mean by offerings? If we read the promise in verse 7, the Lord says: "Return unto me and I will return unto you." He makes it pretty clear that whatever type of offering we sincerely offer to the Lord will be recognized and rewarded. While the specific value and quantity of the reward is undefined, it is certainly sufficient, based on the promise that "there shall not be room enough to receive it." All service we render to the Lord, from the simplest project to the most dedicated offering and sacrifice we can muster, is received by the Lord and blessed. The level of blessing is really up to us when we stop to think about it.

The final verses of Malachi 3 bring up an issue which afflicts almost all people who try to serve the Lord and obey his statutes. Verses 14 and 15 demonstrate that the Lord is aware of this issue; namely, the apparent wealth, prosperity, and happiness of those who pursue worldly pleasure and success rather than follow the Lord's way. He says:

> 14 Ye have said: It is vain to serve God, and what doth it profit that we have kept his ordinances and that we have walked mournfully before the Lord of Hosts?
>
> 15 And now we call the proud happy; yea, they work wickedness and are set up; yea, they that tempt God are even delivered.

It is sometimes very difficult for humble followers of Christ to look all around and see the outward appearances of wealth and success and the apparent joy of men and women who have made mammon their god. It is often tempting to wonder why such people seem to have it all. The big houses the fancy cars, boats, and airplanes, and the stylish clothes—all seem to indicate that those who pursue worldly wealth instead of spiritual strength enjoy more and greater happiness than do those who follow God. This reality is manifest in all ages and times and in every culture. It is the way of the world and always has been since the beginning when Cain slew Abel and took all his possessions. The Nephites were susceptible to this envy as well, and in these verses the Lord addresses the subject. He does not deny that this is a reality. He does not even try to say that those worldly people are not happy, as we often do. They may in fact be very happy according to their own worldly perspective. In Matthew 6:2 the Lord acknowledges that worldly people receive worldly rewards. While speaking about the act of charitable giving the Lord says:

Therefore, when thou doest thine alms, do not sound a trumpet before thee, as the hypocrites do in the synagogues and in the streets, that they may have glory of men. Verily I say unto you, they have their reward. (Matthew 6:2)

It is very possible to be unrighteous and yet have great worldly wealth, power, and prestige. It seems that to get ahead in this world one must play by the rules of this world. That is often true. When Satan was banished from the garden, he was given a degree of dominion over this mortal world. He is called, in 2 Corinthians 4:4, "the god of this world" and was given access to all its riches. He uses those riches now to buy up the hearts and souls of greedy men and women. His message to all is money can buy you anything.

The question then is, "What sort of riches do we want?" We can have our reward now, here on earth if we choose, but how enduring and everlasting is that? The bigger question is, "Do we want some now or more later?" It has always been a temptation for man to take instant gratification over a longer-term reward. It seems more real and tangible, and we are, by nature, impatient. In the end, it becomes a matter of faith. How much faith do we have in the Lord's response to this question, as found in the next three verses?

16 Then they that feared the Lord spake often one to another, and the Lord hearkened and heard; and a book of remembrance was written before him for them that feared the Lord, and that thought upon his name.

17 And they shall be mine, saith the Lord of Hosts, in that day when I make up my jewels; and I will spare them as a man spareth his own son that served him.

18 Then shall ye return and discern between the righteous and the wicked, between him that serveth God and him that serveth him not.

The Lord calls us "jewels" and promises rewards in a heavenly venue where "moth and rust doth not corrupt, and thieves do not break in and steal." The rewards he offers are eternal in nature and will endure as long as the eternal God endures. Satan is god of this mortal world, and his reign lasts only until the end of that mortality. The earth is just about through as a mortal testing ground. It eagerly awaits its own rebirth during the millennial reign, at which time Satan will be bound and will have no more power over the earth or its inhabitants. At that time all who served him will be serving a bankrupt master who cannot pay them their wage and they will be left desolate, jobless, and broke.

The great promise, then, of Malachi 3 is that the Lord is coming back to reclaim his own. The Nephites are part of that group he wishes to reclaim and if they will serve him in righteousness, they will find rewards in heaven and also on the earth. The Lord will be their protector here and will keep the devourer at bay. Once this mortal existence is over, they will find their names written in his book of remembrance and they will find a place in his kingdom, which will endure throughout all eternity.

Malachi 4

The Savior continued his recitation of Malachi in 3 Nephi 25, which contains the text from Malachi 4. The first three verses of this chapter continue the text from the end of Malachi 3 and probably should have been part of that chapter. The balance of this short chapter contains a wonderful promise for the salvation of all generations of time.

This chapter is only six verses long. It contains a curse, a commandment, and a promise. In the Jewish manner of speaking this would be a complete thought and, indeed, the shortness of this chapter belies the power of its message. Starting with the first verse, we find an expansion on the fate of those who choose worldly wealth and pleasure over the ways of the Lord.

> 1 For behold, the day cometh that shall burn as an oven; and all the proud, yea, and all that do wickedly, shall be stubble; and the day that cometh shall burn them up, saith the Lord of Hosts, that it shall leave them neither root nor branch.

The Lord often uses the term stubble to refer to those who do wickedly. In an agrarian society, everyone knows what stubble is. It is the remains of the stalk that is left in the field after the harvest. All the food has been taken from the plant. The corn, wheat, or barley has been reaped and the bare stalk is left. It provides no further use except to be recycled so that its elements might replenish the soil. This is accomplished by burning the fields after the harvest. This clears the field for the planting of a new crop. When the field is burned, "neither root nor branch" is left. So it will be for those who have spent a lifetime storing up earthly treasures. They will awaken to find their treasure as stubble and of no worth anymore.

We get mini-examples of this each time we choose instant gratification over longer-term efforts. The instant gratification of buying some shiny new thing is replaced quickly by the accumulated long-term debt we incur to buy it. Often times we are left with a mountain of debt long after the object of our desire is gone.

The phrase "without root nor branch" also speaks to the reality that those who eschew righteousness and the blessings of the temple will not participate in the sealing ordinances that bind them to both their ancestors and their posterity. They will very literally be left without root nor branch.

This lesson from Malachi had both short-term temporal and long-term spiritual value for the Nephites and also for us today. It is no wonder that the Father commanded Jesus to deliver these words so that they might be added to the records.

The reward for fearing God and giving heed to his commandments comes next.

> 2 But unto you that fear my name, shall the Son of Righteousness arise with healing in his wings; and ye shall go forth and grow up as calves in the stall.
>
> 3 And ye shall tread down the wicked; for they shall be ashes under the soles of your feet in the day that I shall do this, saith the Lord of Hosts.

After this comes a very simple commandment.

> 4 Remember ye the law of Moses, my servant, which I commanded unto him in Horeb for all Israel, with the statutes and judgments.

It is because of the law that these things will all come to pass. Without the law there can be no judgment, for as Nephi said:

> And if ye shall say there is no law, ye shall also say there is no sin. If ye shall say there is no sin, ye shall also say there is no righteousness. And if there be no righteousness there be no happiness. And if there be no righteousness nor happiness there be no punishment nor misery. And if these things are not there is no God. And if there is no God we are not, neither the earth; for there could have been no creation of things, neither to act nor to be acted upon; wherefore, all things must have vanished away. (2 Nephi 2:13)

It was such a simple statement, but it carries such great implications—"remember ye the law of Moses."

We have received, in these four short verses, the curse and the commandment. Now, it is time for the blessing, and the simplicity of the statement might not make the greatness of the blessing readily apparent at first.

> 5 Behold, I will send you Elijah the prophet before the coming of the great and dreadful day of the Lord;
> 6 And he shall turn the heart of the fathers to the children, and the heart of the children to their fathers, lest I come and smite the whole earth with a curse.

To understand this prophecy and promise, we must first understand who Elijah is and why he would be sent before the Second Coming of the Lord.

Elijah

Elijah the Tishbite lived roughly 150 years before Isaiah in the land of Gilead. The title *Tishbite* is a mystery. Researchers have been unable to find any place known by such a name, or reference to anything else that would merit such an appellation. He is revered by the Jews and esteemed by most as their most important prophet. This is primarily for two reasons. Elijah was the one who stood up to the wicked Ahab, king of the Northern Kingdom of Israel, whose evil wife, Jezebel, introduced Ba'al worship to the Jews (1 Kings 18). Because of her patronage of the cults of Ba'al, the Jews of the Northern Kingdom almost completely forsook Jehovah in favor of the Phoenician idol. On one famous occasion, Elijah challenged 450 priests of Ba'al to put their god up against Jehovah (1 Kings 18). Elijah had a bull sacrificed and split it in two, giving the priests one half. He then gave them one day to pray to their god that he might send down fire to consume the offering. After a day filled with rites, ceremonies, sacrifices, and prayer the priests were unsuccessful. Elijah then had the people bring buckets of water which they poured over his portion of the slaughtered bull. Once the offering was completely drenched, he then called down fire from heaven, which completely consumed the offering. The people were so impressed that they gave their allegiance to Elijah, who then commanded them to kill the wicked priests.

On another occasion, Elijah sealed up the heavens and withheld the rain for three and a half years from the Northern Kingdom, and he also made pronouncements about the deaths of Ahab and Jezebel, which ultimately came true.

Elijah is also revered by the Jews because of the promise found here in Malachi 4:5–6. They take the promises made here to indicate that Elijah will return, bringing with him the promised Messiah. To that end, their various rites recognize Elijah as a man of great honor. At the *seder*[1] dinner a place is set for him at every table, along with a special cup of wine. At each *bris*[2] a chair is set aside for his comfort, and at the conclusion of each *Shabbat*,[3] the Jews sing a song about Elijah, expressing the hope that he will "speedily come . . . along with the Messiah, son of David, to redeem us."

The fact that Malachi says the Lord will send Elijah before the great and dreadful day of the Lord is sufficient reason for the Jews to hold him in great honor; yet, that doesn't explain why it was Elijah the Lord would send. One might think the Lord would have sent Moses; after all, Moses was the first great liberator of the Israelites and giver of the law to which all Jews adhere to this day. Why not Abraham, the father of them all and the man who secured the covenant they all claim? Some might have thought Jacob would be a good one to send. As the father of the twelve tribes would it not be appropriate for him, as patriarch, to come and introduce them to their Messiah? These are all good candidates to serve as herald for the Lord, yet Malachi specifically names Elijah as the one to have the honor.

At various times, throughout the Restoration, Joseph Smith was visited by angelic and resurrected beings. After the First Vision, during which Joseph spoke with the Father and the Savior, he was visited by the resurrected Moroni who showed him the location of the golden plates. It was appropriate for Moroni to come, as he was the one who buried them fourteen centuries earlier. It was also appropriate because Moroni held the keys to the Book of Mormon. As the last possessor of the golden plates, it was his responsibility to keep them until they were to be delivered to another. Of course, that other person was Joseph Smith, the translator of the Book of Mormon. Later, Joseph Smith was baptized and ordained to the Aaronic Priesthood by John the Baptist, who held the keys to that priesthood. After him, Joseph was visited by Peter who, along with James and John (the Beloved), held some of the keys to the Melchizedek Priesthood. In each case it was the holder of the keys whom the Lord sent to restore the various aspects of the gospel to Joseph. Part of their assignment was to confer those keys to him. We are taught that Joseph and all the subsequent prophets since him hold all the keys of the gospel. They serve as stewards of those keys until they are passed on to others upon their death. Ultimately, those keys will all be returned to Adam, who, as the patriarch of us all, will return them to the Savior as he begins his millennial reign.

Elijah was the last prophet of the past dispensation to hold all of the keys of the priesthood. It was he who appeared, along with Moses, to Peter, James, and John on the Mount of Transfiguration. There he conferred the keys of the priesthood to the three apostles, who were to carry on the work of the Lord after his crucifixion. However, Peter, James, and John did not get all of the keys of the Melchizedek Priesthood. This is because there was not, nor would there be thereafter, a functioning temple in which the sealing ordinances of the everlasting gospel could be performed. They were given the keys to administer in the Melchizedek Priesthood, ordaining others and performing miracles through the gifts of the Spirit and the priesthood power. Their mission was to organize and build the Church, issuing callings and establishing branches of the Church throughout their world. They received all the keys necessary for that, but Elijah held on to the keys of the sealing powers and the temple ordinances.

It was Peter, James, and John who conferred the Melchizedek Priesthood to Joseph and Oliver, rather than Elijah, because at that time their keys were all the keys Joseph and Oliver needed to establish the Church. As the Church grew and the time came for temples to once again grace the land, Joseph needed the additional keys pertaining to those holy ordinances.

In the following excerpt from a talk read at General Conference on October 5, 1840, Joseph Smith speaks of Elijah. He says:

> Elijah was the last prophet that held the keys of the Priesthood, and who will, before the last dispensation, restore the authority and deliver the keys of the Priesthood, in order that all the ordinances may be attended to in righteousness. It is true that the Savior had authority and power to bestow this blessing; but the sons of Levi were too prejudiced. "And I will send Elijah the Prophet before the great and terrible day of the Lord," etc. etc. Why send Elijah? Because he holds the keys of the authority to administer in all the ordinances of the Priesthood;

and without the authority given, the ordinances could not be administered in righteousness.[4]

Elijah held the keys to the sealing power. Whatsoever thing he sealed on earth was sealed in heaven. He demonstrated this power to Ahab when he sealed the heavens and stopped the rain for the space of three and a half years. When he called down fire from heaven to consume the bull, it came. This sealing power had far greater uses than to chastise wicked rulers, however. Elijah's keys of sealing held the power to bind families together throughout eternity. He had the power to bind families on earth and have them bound for eternity in heaven. He held the keys to all of the temple ordinances that perform such work. At the funeral of Judge Elias Higbee, held at Nauvoo on August 13, 1843, Joseph spoke once again of Elijah:

> He shall send Elijah the prophet, and he shall reveal the covenants of the fathers in relation to the children, and the covenants of the children in relation to the fathers.[5]

William Clayton reported that on that same occasion, Joseph said the following, referring to Elijah: "When speaking of the passage, 'I will send Elijah the prophet, etc.,' it should read, 'And he shall turn the hearts of the children to the covenant made with their fathers.' "[6]

Then, just a few months later, while giving a sermon on the Sabbath, Joseph taught the following:

> The Bible says, "I will send you Elijah the Prophet before the coming of the great and dreadful day of the Lord; and he shall turn the hearts of the fathers to the children, and the hearts of the children to the fathers, lest I come and smite the earth with a curse."
>
> Now, the word "turn" here should be translated bind, or seal. But what is the object of this important mission? Or, how is it to be fulfilled? The keys are to be delivered, the spirit of Elijah is to come, the gospel is to be established, the Saints of God gathered, Zion built up, and the Saints to come up as saviors on Mount Zion.[7]

He followed up this sermon with another, just six weeks later, during which he said:

> Now for Elijah. The spirit, power, and calling of Elijah is that ye have power to hold the key of the revelation, ordinances, oracles, powers and the endowments of the fulness of the Melchizedek Priesthood and

the kingdom of God on the earth; to receive, obtain, and perform all the ordinances belonging to the kingdom of God, even unto the turning of the hearts of the fathers unto the children, and the hearts of the children unto the fathers, even those who are in heaven.

Now comes the point. What is this office and work of Elijah? It is one of the greatest and most important subjects that God has revealed? He should send Elijah to seal the children to the fathers, and the fathers to the children.

I wish you to understand this subject, for it is important; and if you will receive it, this is the spirit of Elijah, that we redeem our dead, and connect ourselves with our fathers which are in heaven, and seal up our dead to come forth in the first resurrection; and here we want the power of Elijah to seal those who dwell on earth to those who dwell in heaven. This is the power of Elijah and the keys of the kingdom of Jehovah.

Then what you seal on earth, by the keys of Elijah, is sealed in heaven.[8]

This visit by Elijah, as mentioned by Malachi, was so important that Moroni, the first visitor Joseph Smith received after his initial visit with the Father and the Son, mentioned it during his three visits in the middle of the night on September 21, 1823. An account of this is found in the Pearl of Great Price, Joseph Smith—History 1:36–39.

After telling me these things, he commenced quoting the prophecies of the Old Testament. He first quoted part of the third chapter of Malachi; and he quoted also the fourth or last chapter of the same prophecy, though with a little variation from the way it read in our Bibles. Instead of quoting the first verse as it reads in our books, he quoted it thus:

For behold, the day cometh that shall burn as an oven, and all the proud, yea, and all that do wickedly shall burn as stubble; for they that come shall burn them, saith the Lord of Hosts, that it shall leave them neither root nor branch.

And again he quoted the fifth verse thus: Behold, I will reveal unto you the Priesthood, by the hand of Elijah the prophet, before the great and dreadful day of the Lord.

He also quoted the next verse differently: And he shall plant in the hearts of the children the promises made to the fathers, and the hearts of the children shall turn to their fathers. If it were not so, the whole earth would be utterly wasted at his coming.

It is interesting to note that Moroni quoted to Joseph Smith the same passages that the Savior quoted to the Nephites. Obviously, for all that the gospel encompasses, all the ordinances and all the doctrines it provides, as valuable as they are, are nothing without the sealing ordinances of the temple, and without those the whole experience of this earth would have been utterly wasted. The purpose of restoring the gospel on the earth before the Savior returned was specifically to set in place temples and their saving ordinances, to lay a foundation for righteousness and establish a chain of connected families and generations ready for the resurrection.

It is no wonder that the Father would command the Savior to place these words among the Nephites.

Notes

1. Jewish ritual feast held on the first night of the Jewish holiday of Passover (the 15th day of the Hebrew month of *Nisan*).
2. The *bris* is a ritual circumcision performed by a *Mohel* usually on the eighth day after birth. It was a symbol of one who was under the covenant of Abraham.
3. *Shabbat* is simply the Jewish Sabbath. It begins at sundown on Friday night and lasts until three stars are visible on Saturday night. The Shabbat feast recognizes the end of the Sabbath day.
4. *History of the Church,* 4:211.
5. *History of the Church,* 5:530.
6. Ibid.
7. Sabbath Address, Nauvoo, 21 January 1844.
8. Sabbath Address, Nauvoo, 10 March 1844.

10

THE SERMON ON THE MOUNT

The Sermon on the Mount is probably the single most important doctrinal summary from the Savior that we have. It was delivered early in his ministry and served as an introduction to the law of Christ, which was intended to supplant the law of Moses as the governing rule for the Jews. When the Savior made his glorious visit to the American continent, the first thing he did, after choosing his twelve Nephite disciples, was deliver another "Sermon on the Mount" to the Nephites.

This passage marks the third type of Biblical scripture we have encountered in the Book of Mormon. Initially, we looked at the writings of Isaiah. These were scriptures copied from transcripts of the Biblical text that Nephi rescued from the hands of Laban before leaving Jerusalem. They are basically verbatim biblical texts found in the Book of Mormon. The differences between the Book of Mormon version and the version found in our Bible highlight the differences in translation and demonstrate the value of finding the purest text with the fewest translations behind it.

The second type of scriptures we studied are those found in 2 Nephi 27 and Isaiah 29. In this case we find two sets of scripture that contain the same prophecy, but which were delivered by two different prophets. The relative fulness of the Nephite version over the Isaiah text may demonstrate how the Lord modifies his message to fit the needs of the people, or it could indicate the relative value of the message to the one group over the other.

The Sermon on the Mount is unique because, as found in the pages of

3 Nephi, it is not expressly a biblical scripture. It is, in fact, the same message, delivered by the same person, but to two different groups of people in two different settings and under two very different circumstances. The version delivered in Jerusalem to the twelve disciples was given before the Crucifixion and Atonement while the version spoken to the Nephite masses was given after the Atonement and Resurrection.

Though not expressly a copy of a biblical transcript, I feel the inclusion of the Nephite version of the Sermon on the Mount in this study of biblical scriptures is justified because the commonality of the two transcripts is such that they can be considered essentially the same. The details do vary, which would be consistent for a talk given to two very different civilizations. In fact, in this case, if the two records were verbatim we might take that as a sign of fraudulent presentation or plagiarism on the part of Joseph Smith.

I have taken great pains in this book to show that the copying of Isaiah and Malachi in the Book of Mormon was completely appropriate and that their words were absolutely applicable to the one group as to the other. With regard to the text of the Sermon on the Mount, however, the same text would not be appropriate for both groups. This is partly because the Jerusalem version was delivered in a private setting, to the twelve disciples only, for the purpose of training them to teach, while the Nephite version was delivered as sort of a general conference talk, addressed to the masses. Also, the Sermon on the Mount was delivered at the beginning of the Savior's three-year ministry, whereas the Book of Mormon version was delivered at its end, after his glorious resurrection.

Matthew's record of the Sermon on the Mount appears just after Jesus had called his disciples to the work. The record indicates that the Lord, seeing the multitudes of people coming to seek him out, gathered his disciples to him and delivered this talk to them, teaching them the gospel so that they could handle the teaching of the multitudes (Matthew 5:1–2).

The Nephites were in a different situation. They had been taught about the Savior for six hundred years and looked forward to his coming from that time on. They had accepted him and already practiced many aspects of his gospel. Nephi records the people's anticipation of the Lord as early as 559 BC:

> And, notwithstanding we believe in Christ, we keep the law of Moses, and look forward with steadfastness unto Christ, until the law shall be fulfilled.

> For, for this purpose was the law given; wherefore the law hath
> become dead unto us, and we are made alive in Christ because of our
> faith; yet we keep the law because of the commandments.
>
> And we talk of Christ, we rejoice in Christ, we preach of Christ,
> we prophesy of Christ, and we write according to our prophecies, that
> our children may know to what source they may look for a remission of
> their sins. (2 Nephi 25:24–26)

Because the people were already aware of most of the elements of
the law of Christ, the Lord did not need to limit his sermon to just
those chosen few disciples who would carry it forth. He was able to
address the assembled multitudes who anxiously awaited his words,
confirming the things they had been taught for six hundred years.

In Matthew, the Sermon on the Mount is one of the first things
spoken by the Savior after he officially began his ministry. In the Book
of Mormon, the Savior appeared gloriously, descending from the heavens
bathed in glory and light, as a resurrected being, having completed his
mission and accomplishing his atoning sacrifice. After his Father's voice
introduced him, Jesus spoke to the amazed throng, beckoning each of
them to come up and feel the wounds in his hands and in his side. Then,
as in Jerusalem, he called disciples, twelve in total, and ordained them,
giving them instructions regarding baptism and the law of his gospel. In
3 Nephi 12:1, we see what happened next:

> Behold, he stretched forth his hand unto the multitude, and cried
> unto them, saying: Blessed are ye if ye shall give heed unto the words of
> the twelve whom I have chosen from among you to minister unto you,
> and to be your servants; and unto them I have given power that they
> may baptize you with water; and after that ye are baptized with water,
> behold I will baptize you with fire and with the Holy Ghost; therefore
> blessed are ye if ye shall believe in me and be baptized, after that ye
> have seen me and know that I am.

As we compare the two sermons and look at the differences between
them, we should remember that this Nephite audience included the whole
mass of inhabitants rather than just the twelve disciples. Additionally, the
Gospel of Matthew was most probably written originally in Aramaic, and
then later translated to Greek, from which we get the version found in
the King James version of the Bible. This transliteration of the text could
have led to some loss, so we should expect a richer text from the Nephite

version. We will put the two accounts side by side for comparison, putting the Matthew account on the left and the 3 Nephi account on the right.

The Beatitudes

The Sermon on the Mount begins with the Beatitudes, which are declarations of the blessedness that accompany certain aspects of righteous living. They set forth the attributes of a true Christian and present the essence of Christlike behavior. Both the Sermon on the Mount and the Sermon in the Americas reveal the characteristics that bring us to Christ, but we can see that in some of the declarations, the Book of Mormon version gives more clarity and detail as to the nature of those characteristics. Let's look at the first one.

3 Nephi 12:3

Mathew 5:3

3 Yea, blessed are the poor in spirit **who come unto me**, for theirs is the kingdom of heaven.

3 Blessed are the poor in spirit: for theirs is the kingdom of heaven.

There are many in the world who are poor in spirit. In fact, almost everybody in the world is poor in spirit. We have spent this entire study reading what Isaiah and Malachi spoke of those with little faith and less integrity. The Book of Mormon devotes one-third of its text to wars and contentions to show the affect of multitudes of people who were poor in spirit. Being poor in spirit is the same as being spiritually lacking. There is nothing noble about being poor in spirit, and it is obviously not a Christlike quality. Somehow, the Matthew version still conveys the essence of the message because we just naturally assume that it is referring to people with humility. However, that is not what it says, and it is just lucky that readers find the essence in spite of the message of the translation. The 3 Nephi version is clear and concise. The addition of the qualifier "who come unto me" differentiates between those who wallow in their spiritual desert and those who humble themselves and come to the Lord. Those are the ones who are blessed and those are the ones who shall inherit the kingdom of heaven.

The fourth beatitude is also slightly different, with one significant addition.

3 Nephi 12:6

6 And blessed are **all** they who do hunger and thirst after righteousness, for they shall be filled **with the Holy Ghost**.

Matthew 5:12

6 Blessed are they which do hunger and thirst after righteousness: for they shall be filled.

The Jews in Jerusalem made the mistake of thinking that righteousness was the same as obedience. To them, the mere compliance with the mandates of the law of Moses was sufficient to satisfy their obligation to be good Jews. The Savior often made the point that obedience, if it was rendered grudgingly or without the consent of the heart, was not righteousness. It is a point he will make later in this sermon. The Holy Ghost is the member of the Godhead who testifies of truth and who seals those truths in our hearts. He teaches us truth and dispels falsehood, filling our bodies with light and purity. He will only come when we act with true, sincere, righteous desire, and when he does come, our thirsting and hungering is sated through the peace he places in our hearts.

The other six beatitudes are recorded alike in both records. They state that people are blessed when they mourn, are meek, are merciful, have a pure heart, are peacemakers, and when they are persecuted and reviled for the sake of the Lord. These are all signs of someone who has found peace in the Lord and who will be humble enough to be led by the Spirit. These are the types of people who would do no harm in the world. If the Nephites and the Lamanites could have embodied more of these qualities wars would have disappeared and peace would have settled over the land. The people would have enjoyed a constant condition of happiness and joy. This fact is demonstrated by the two generations that follow the Lord's visit to the Americas. Their blissful state is directly attributable to their adoption of the qualities espoused in the Beatitudes.

Salt

The use of salt as an image in the Sermon on the Mount is tied to the very ancient "Covenant of Salt," as mentioned in Numbers 18 and 2 Chronicles 13. It was a covenant of "perpetual obligation," which reminded the Israelites of the eternal nature of their obligation and bond with the Lord. The salt represented purifying and preserving and referred to the purifying that the house of Israel could bring to the rest of the world through the gospel and priesthood that it bore.

In ancient days salt was extremely valuable and absolutely essential for the survival of man in most parts of the world.[1] Its ability to allow food to dry without putrefaction allowed people to put up and store large amounts of food against famine. Fish (another strong symbol of the Middle East) was especially perishable and could not be stored or dried without salt. Salt also allowed people to survive in arid regions without excessive dehydration.

The preserving aspect of salt symbolized the protective nature of the Lord's watchful eye over all who follow him and keep his commandments, and his promise that he would protect and preserve them. In recognition of the covenant of salt, Israelite children were rubbed with salt at birth.

Jews at the time of Jesus' earthly mission were acquainted with the covenant of salt though its rigid observation had diminished over the years. As a result, the next part of his sermon was touching, familiar territory for them.

3 Nephi 12:13

13 **Verily, verily, I say unto you, I give unto you to be** the salt of the earth; but if the salt shall lose its savor wherewith shall the earth be salted? **The salt shall be** thenceforth good for nothing, but to be cast out and to be trodden under foot of men.

Matthew 5:13

13 Ye are the salt of the earth: but if the salt have lost his savour, wherewith shall it be salted? it is thenceforth good for nothing, but to be cast out, and to be trodden under foot of men.

The twelve disciples in Jerusalem were familiar with the old Hebrew covenants and imagery concerning salt. The Lord could say to them, "Ye are the salt of the earth" and they understood what that meant. On the other hand, none of the Book of Mormon prophets had taught their people much of the ways of the Jews. Therefore, the Savior's statement to the Nephites that, "I give unto you to be the salt of the earth," was issued more as a calling than as a declarative statement. This also demonstrated the concept of agency by indicating that the Nephites had a choice in choosing to follow the Lord and serve him.

This same "calling vs. statement" shows up in the next verse.

3 Nephi 12:14	Matthew 5:14
14 **Verily, verily, I say unto you, I give unto you to be the light of this people**. A city that is set on a hill cannot be hid.	14 Ye are the light of the world. A city that is set on an hill cannot be hid.

In the first case we have the Lord saying that the people are "the light of the world," while in the other he says: "I give unto you to be *the light of this people*." The people of Jerusalem were responsible for the New Testament, a book that truly went out as a light to the world and helped the spread of Christianity to every nation. The Nephite people, on the other hand, did not get to contribute to that great work with any of their own words or testimony due to their isolation. Their message to the world would have to come later. It would become a second witness, which, we now know as the Book of Mormon. The Book of Mormon is the voice of this people, and the testimony of this very event—that is, the visit of the Savior to the Americas—is one of the primary elements of it. Moroni's own words in the title page state that one of the principle reasons for the Book of Mormon is for the convincing of the Jew and the Gentile that Jesus is the Christ. In a very real way, the people attending this historic event are the light of the Nephites. Their testimony of the Savior's visit gives the Book of Mormon its power and message to the world.

Moving on to verse 18 we find a subtle difference that is very significant.

3 Nephi 12:18	Matthew 5:18
18 For verily I say unto you, one jot nor one tittle **hath not** passed away from the law, but in me **it hath all been** fulfilled.	18 For verily I say unto you, Till heaven and earth pass, one jot or one tittle **shall in no wise** pass from the law, **till all be** fulfilled.

In the Biblical version the Lord is speaking of the future. He is saying that the law remains in effect and each and every element of it is still valid, and will remain so, until it is fulfilled. The Atonement in the garden and the subsequent Crucifixion on Golgotha were to be that fulfillment. Once the great sacrifice was made the law of Moses would be supplanted by the law of Christ. As the Savior spoke these words to his disciples in Jerusalem, that had not yet happened. However, in the New World, as he spoke to the Nephites, the sacrifice had already taken place and the law had been fulfilled. It was therefore very proper to speak in the past tense, declaring that "it hath all been fulfilled," rather than continue to use the future tense as he had in Jerusalem.

Once again, in verses 19 and 20, we see significant variation that plays to the differences between the two audiences.

3 Nephi 12:19–20	Matthew 5:19–20
19 **And behold, I have given you the law and the commandments of my Father, that ye shall believe in me, and that ye shall repent of your sins, and come unto me with a broken heart and a contrite spirit. Behold, ye have the commandments before you, and the law is fulfilled.**	19 Whosoever therefore shall break one of these least commandments, and shall teach men so, he shall be called the least in the kingdom of heaven: but whosoever shall do and teach them, the same shall be called great in the kingdom of heaven.
20 **Therefore come unto me and be ye saved**; for verily I say unto you, that except **ye shall keep my commandments, which I have commanded you at this time**, ye shall in no case enter into the kingdom of heaven.	20 For I say unto you, That except your righteousness shall exceed the righteousness of the scribes and Pharisees, ye shall in no case enter into the kingdom of heaven.

We find here basically two different sets of verses that convey the same message. Again we may attribute part of the difference to the fact that in the one instance the law had yet to be fulfilled while in the other it was already fulfilled. However, there is another very interesting omission in the Book of Mormon text that would be inappropriate were it to appear there. It is the reference to the scribes and Pharisees in Matthew 5:20.

Scribes and Pharisees were political positions that grew out of the subjugation of the Jews by other nations. They are not offices of the priesthood and were not part of the Jewish faith at the time Lehi and his family left Jerusalem. By about 200 BC they had replaced the Levite priests as administrators of the law. They took upon themselves the title of Rabbi, or teacher (another title not found in ancient Israelite tradition), and became the masters of the law of Moses. It was they to whom the people looked for interpretation and clarification of the law whenever there was a dispute. To our knowledge, the people of Lehi had no understanding of the terms *scribe* or *Pharisee*. They had never heard these terms before, and their reference in this sermon would have been confusing and of no value whatsoever. Had the Book of Mormon included these words, we would have been justified in being suspicious of the validity of this translation.

General Points of Christianity

The Sermon on the Mount is organized in the following manner. It begins with a statement of hope and simplicity, showing the attributes of a blessed people. Its simple declarative is that humility, and the traits that accompany it, is the essence of the secret for finding peace both here on earth and in heaven. The Beatitudes list those qualities and show the blessings associated with each one. Next comes the "mission statement" issuing a calling to the people, or rather, revealing their pre-existing calling to be a beacon to the world and a source to which the people of the world can look for salvation and the blessings of God. After that the Lord spells out the basic rules of Christianity and, in some cases, shows the differences between the law of Christ and the law of Moses. After these things are presented, the Lord concludes with promises of salvation to those who follow him and accept these things.

The Sermon on the Mount is filled with rich doctrine and great blessings. It would be well to study the entire text in depth; however, we are primarily focusing on a comparison between the two texts of this great speech and studying the differences. To that end we must pass by rich gems and move forward.

One of the early differences we encounter addresses our ability to come unto God while we are angry with our brother.

3 Nephi 12:23–24

23 Therefore, if ye shall **come unto me, or shall desire to come unto me**, and rememberest that thy brother hath aught against thee—

24 Go thy way unto thy brother, and first be reconciled to thy brother, and then come **unto me with full purpose of heart, and I will receive you.**

Matthew 5:23–24

23 Therefore if thou **bring thy gift to the altar**, and there rememberest that thy brother hath ought against thee;

24 **Leave there thy gift before the altar**, and go thy way; first be reconciled to thy brother, and then come and offer thy gift.

As we look at these passages we immediately see one difference, which at first glance doesn't seem so significant. In the Biblical text the circumstance is one of bringing an offering to the altar of the temple or tabernacle. In the Book of Mormon, however, the action is the bringing of oneself to God directly. While this may not seem significant, it in fact speaks volumes. Within the law of Moses, the worship of the Lord was accomplished through the giving of offerings and sacrifices. These things were done in very ceremonial fashion with each action carefully prescribed and each step followed exactly. In many instances the offerings were brought to the priest, who performed the sacrifice for the family. He also acted as an intercessor for the individual or family, to convey their message to Jehovah for them. The people did not plead directly with the Lord save through these means. Remember, the Savior had not yet fulfilled the law of Moses, and the requirements of that law still required sacrifices and offerings. These were acts that could be complied with without having any real inner desire or personal yearning. Simple obedience was enough. The concept of a personal relationship with God was unknown.

Speaking to the Nephites, however, the Lord had already fulfilled the law of Moses, and the requirement for blood sacrifices was done away with. The Lamb had been slain and the Atonement was complete. There would be no more offerings upon the altars in similitude of the promised Lamb of God. Under the law of Christ, people were expected to develop a personal relationship with the Lord. Simple mechanical compliance with the statutes was not enough. The intent of the heart was the determining factor in judging a person's sincerity. In return for developing this personal relationship, the people had the ability to seek him, praying and communicating directly with him rather than through a priest. So we find in 3 Nephi the Savior saying, "If ye shall come unto me, or desire to come unto me," and a verse later, "Then come unto me . . . and I will receive you." The fact that there is no mention of altars or gifts simply recognizes that those times are past.

The next few verses speak to the wisdom of settling disputes quickly. While the text is similar and the council the same, the use of the different monetary units is interesting.

3 Nephi 12:25–26	Matthew 5:25–26
25 Agree with thine adversary quickly while thou art in the way with him, lest at any time he shall get thee, and thou shalt be cast into prison. 26 Verily, verily, I say unto thee, thou shalt by no means come out thence until thou hast paid the uttermost **senine. And while ye are in prison can ye pay even one senine? Verily, verily, I say unto you, Nay.**	25 Agree with thine adversary quickly, whiles thou art in the way with him; lest at any time the adversary deliver thee **to the judge, and the judge deliver thee to the officer**, and thou be cast into prison. 26 Verily I say unto thee, Thou shalt by no means come out thence, till thou hast paid the uttermost farthing.

A farthing was a unit of Jewish money worth about one-sixteenth of a Roman "denarius" or penny. Coins did not appear in the Jewish monetary system until after their exposure to the Persian Empire of Darius the Great. That occurred after they were taken captive by Nebuchadnezzar and the Babylonians in 592 BC, which was eight years after Lehi and his family left Jerusalem. Therefore, it would have been impossible for the Nephites to know what a "farthing" was. They would have had no reference for knowing what a farthing was or that it was the very smallest amount of money in Jewish society.

Alma 11 explains the Nephite coinage and shows that in their society, the senine was the smallest unit of money used among the Nephites (Alma 11:6–19). In both scriptures the Lord simply used the smallest coin known to the people to illustrate that even the smallest debt could not be paid while in prison.

As he continues his sermon, the Lord speaks of the sin of adultery and shows the people the higher principle of compliance he expects. This is the same in both versions. However, his rationale for expecting the higher standard is explained differently for the two audiences.

3 Nephi 12:29–30	Matthew 5:29–30
29 **Behold, I give unto you a commandment, that ye suffer none of these things to enter into your heart;** 30 **For it is better that ye should**	29 And if thy right eye offend thee, pluck it out, and cast it from thee: for it is profitable for thee that one of thy members should perish, and not that thy whole body should be cast into hell. 30 And if thy right hand offend

| deny yourselves of these things, wherein ye will take up your cross, than that ye should be cast into hell. | thee, cut it off, and cast it from thee: for it is profitable for thee that one of thy members should perish, and not that thy whole body should be cast into hell. |

We find a completely different tone in the Book of Mormon from that found in the Bible. Once again we see that the Lord knew his audience and spoke to their experience. Jews and Arabs alike, and all Middle Eastern people for that matter, were of the belief that individual members of the body were responsible for their actions. Paul spoke of his members as being at war with his mind, and implied that he thought of them as being almost separate from the real him. In Romans 7:23 he said,

> But I see another law in my members, warring against the law of my mind, and bringing me into captivity to the law of sin which is in my members.

Criminal justice still reflects this mentality in some countries to this day. In many Arabic countries, a thief is still punished by having his right hand cut off. In speaking to the twelve disciples in Jerusalem, the Lord did not intend to tell them that they should literally pluck out their eyes or cut off other members of their body. He knew that they would understand the meaning of his words and could relate them to their existing justice system. He was making a point and speaking according to the tradition of the day to get that point across.

On the other hand, the Nephites viewed weakness as a matter of personal integrity. Nephi shows us this in 2 Nephi 4:18–19 when he takes responsibility for his own weaknesses. He says:

> I am encompassed about because of the temptations and the sins which do so easily beset me.
> And when I desire to rejoice, my heart groaneth because of my sins; nevertheless, I know in whom I have trusted.

We see here a man, well aware of the weakness within him. He takes responsibility for his sins and does not try to detach himself from them. He says: "which do so easily beset *me*," and "because of *my* sins." There is no evidence that the Nephites employed the same detachment from their sins nor the harsh "eye for an eye" type of punishment in their legal system as did the Jews. True they were Semites, and they had the law of Moses, and the history of the Israelites down to Jeremiah, but, as they had been looking forward to Christ for six hundred years and had adopted many more "Christian" ideas during that time, it seems they had blended the harsh Mosaic code with some of the mercy and forgiveness that came with Christianity.

In trying to make the same point to them as he had made to the disciples in Jerusalem, the Lord spoke to the Nephites on a different level. For one thing, he mentioned their hearts and said: "Suffer none of these things to enter your heart." He also spoke of self-denial and even touched upon a higher idea by indicating that by exercising such restraint and denying themselves worldly pleasures for righteousness sake, they could be more like him by taking up their own cross.

Continuing on we find the Savior speaking of swearing, or foreswearing—that is, making oaths. He says:

3 Nephi 12:35	Matthew 5:35
35 Nor by the earth, for it is his footstool;	35 Nor by the earth; for it is his footstool: **neither by Jerusalem; for it is the city of the great King**.

The omission of the reference to Jerusalem here is not surprising. The Lord did not use Jerusalem in his edict to the Nephites simply because it belonged to another people in another place. Because of their history, the Nephites at the meridian of time knew of Jerusalem, but the great city did not have the significance to them like it did to the Jews in Jerusalem. There would have been no temptation for them to swear by Jerusalem.

In the next few verses we see another example of the Lord acknowledging the differences between the people and the lands that they inhabited.

3 Nephi 12:45	Matthew 5:45
45 That ye may be the children of your Father who is in heaven; for he maketh his sun to rise on the evil and on the good.	45 That ye may be the children of your Father which is in heaven: for he maketh his sun to rise on the evil and on the good, **and sendeth rain on the just and on the unjust.**

The people of Israel lived in an arid land where every drop of rain that fell was considered a blessing from God. People prayed for rain constantly and uttered prayers of gratitude to the Lord when if fell. We have already seen, in the Old Testament, the story of Elijah sealing up the heavens and holding the rain at bay for three and a half years. We also have the story of Joseph gaining favor with Pharaoh by correctly predicting and preparing for the seven-year drought and ensuing famine, thus saving the Egyptians as well as his own family. Conversely, the people of the New World lived in a tropical and verdant setting. Rain was as common as trees and plants and the abundant life all around. While it certainly was always a blessing to have rain, the Nephites would not have considered rain as anything more than just one of the constituent elements of their land. Using rain as an example of a blessing would have had no more effect than mentioning the soil under their feet.

After the preceding verses the Lord finishes these thoughts with two completely different remarks.

3 Nephi 12:46–48

46 **Therefore those things which were of old time, which were under the law, in me are all fulfilled.**

47 **Old things are done away, and all things have become new.**

48 Therefore **I would that** ye should be perfect **even as I**, or your Father who is in heaven is perfect.

Matthew 5:46–48

46 For if ye love them which love you, what reward have ye? do not even the publicans the same?

47 And if ye salute your brethren only, what do ye more than others? do not even the publicans so?

48 Be ye therefore perfect, even as your Father which is in heaven is perfect.

At the beginning of his ministry, the Savior was giving his new disciples advice and insight as to how he wanted them to treat all the people, not just their friends and allies. He concluded with the command to strive for perfection, as their Father in Heaven was perfect. In the New World, the Savior made a different statement. He flatly declared that the old law was fulfilled. It was done away with and a new law was in its place. Though he didn't specifically say it (at least, it is not indicated in our records), a new dispensation had commenced with the establishment of the new law. In Jerusalem, the Savior, though he lived perfectly, was not yet perfected. He had not made his atonement nor had he yet fulfilled his mission. It was, therefore, appropriate that he should command his disciples to be perfect as his Father was perfect. By the time he arrived in the Americas, the man Jesus had become the Savior. He had completed the Atonement, and he had been resurrected. He had become a perfected being. For this reason he could say, to the Nephites, "Be ye therefore perfect even as I, or your Father, is perfect."

The Lord uses the Sermon on the Mount to teach all of his disciples the proper manner of prayer. He begins Matthew 6 and 3 Nephi 13 by explaining the humility that should be displayed and the sacred nature of true prayer. His council is good for both audiences and his teachings are the same. In general, the Bible and the Book of Mormon texts are remarkably similar. The Savior shows the manner of prayer that he would like his followers to employ. He gives an example.

3 Nephi 13:9–11	Matthew 6:9–12
9 After this manner therefore pray ye: Our Father who art in heaven, hallowed be thy name.	9 After this manner therefore pray ye: Our Father which art in heaven, Hallowed be thy name.
10 Thy will be done on earth as it is in heaven.	10 **Thy kingdom come.** Thy will be done in earth, as it is in heaven.
	11 **Give us this day our daily bread.**
11 And forgive us our debts, as we forgive our debtors.	12 And forgive us our debts, as we forgive our debtors.

Right away we see two omissions in the Book of Mormon version of these passages. Verse 10 of 3 Nephi 13 omits the plea "thy kingdom come," and it completely skips Matthew's verse 11 which says, "Give us this day our daily bread," going instead, straight to "forgive us our debts." These omissions are not accidental.

When Jesus spoke to the disciples in Jerusalem, he was just setting about to establish the kingdom of heaven on earth. It had not yet been established, and it was completely appropriate for him to ask all his disciples to plead for its advent. However, by the time he visited the Nephites, he had established his kingdom on earth. The priesthood resided with the apostles, and the Church had a basic footing and structure. Sadly, the Apostasy would come along shortly to corrupt the gospel, but Christianity would, nevertheless, be established, and though it would take on many different and erroneous forms, it would lay the foundation for the Restoration and the fulness of the gospel in the latter days. It would have been odd for the Savior to teach the Nephites to plead for something that had already happened, so it was appropriate that he omitted that particular phrase for his prayer.

The reason for the omission of the supplication "give us this day our daily bread" is a little bit more obscure. To understand this we need to know something about the lives of the disciples. The first thing we need to remember is that the twelve disciples, to whom the Savior addressed these words, were called and set apart for full-time service in his work. We can read his instructions to them regarding their work in Matthew 10:

> 6. But go rather to the lost sheep of the house of Israel.
> 7. And as ye go, preach, saying, The kingdom of heaven is at hand.
> 8. Heal the sick, cleanse the lepers, raise the dead, cast out devils: freely ye have received, freely give.
> 9. Provide neither gold, nor silver, nor brass in your purses,
> 10. Nor scrip for your journey, neither two coats, neither shoes, nor yet staves: for the workman is worthy of his meat.

The edict to go forth without purse or scrip, and to rely on the Lord for all their needs was fundamental to their calling. It was, therefore, appropriate that they should remember to ask the Lord for their daily bread. On the other hand, when addressing the Nephites, the Lord was speaking to people who worked every day for their sustenance. Even their leaders prided themselves on the fact that they toiled with their own hands for their own support so that they wouldn't be an undue burden to the people. King Benjamin told his people:

> And even I, myself, have labored with mine own hands that I might serve you, and that ye should not be laden with taxes, and that there should nothing come upon you which was grievous to be borne. (Mosiah 2:14)

Though the Lord was addressing the general population of the Nephite, and shaping his words to their circumstances, he did, nevertheless, call and set apart twelve disciples for them as well. These twelve needed special instructions that pertained to them specifically. Therefore, the Lord set aside his remarks to the general population for a moment and spoke to his disciples privately. As he directed his remarks directly to them, he sounded again as he had in Jerusalem. He gave them instructions for living their lives without purse or scrip while in his exclusive service. 3 Nephi 13:25 says:

And now it came to pass that when Jesus had spoken these words
he looked upon the twelve whom he had chosen, and said unto them:
Remember the words which I have spoken. For behold, ye are they
whom I have chosen to minister unto this people. Therefore I say unto
you, take no thought for your life, what ye shall eat, or what ye shall
drink; nor yet for your body, what ye shall put on. Is not the life more
than meat, and the body than raiment?

At this point the Lord gives them the same direction he gave his
twelve back in Jerusalem. All the attributes of one who labors full time in
the Lord's service are explained. Much of this same advice is issued today
to the thousands of missionaries who leave their homes and their lives for
full-time missionary service.

The Lord then turns his attention back to the multitude to finish his
thoughts.

This ten-verse pause, where Jesus stops to speak privately to his Nephite
disciples, is important. Had the record in 3 Nephi simply continued on
without the pause, as it does in Matthew, we probably never would have
noticed the inconsistency. Yet, the constancy of the presentation serves as
a powerful testimony to the fact that this record is a true and authentic
transcript of words actually spoken by the Savior to the Nephites after his
resurrection.

As with all the biblical scriptures we have compared from the Book of
Mormon, the Sermon on the Mount comparison serves to show that the
record of the Book of Mormon is unique and authentic.

Conclusion

We have studied subtleties that have taken scholars years to recognize.
We have found differences that at the time of Joseph Smith may have
appeared to be errors but which, when further discoveries were made,
suddenly seemed remarkably insightful.

It has always been tempting for critics of Joseph Smith and the
Church, to dismiss the Book of Mormon as first, an outright lie, and
second, a device to "Mormonize" Christianity and justify our own pecu-
liar doctrines. In this they err, for what is often overlooked is the fact that
when the Book of Mormon was first published and presented to the world
there were no peculiarly Mormon doctrines to defend. In 1830 we had no
doctrine of multiple kingdoms of heaven, no doctrine of the premortal
life. There were no apostles, stakes, wards, or priesthood quorums. We did

not have temples nor their ordinances. The prophecy about Elijah, found in the Book of Mormon as well as in Malachi, had yet to be fulfilled. We did not have the Word of Wisdom or a doctrine about polygamy. In short, in 1830 the Church was very little more than a small group of men who, having come from Protestant backgrounds, found themselves with a new book of scripture and a young man who said an angel gave it to him to translate. To claim that in such a circumstance, a young, uneducated boy could have woven together such a story as the Book of Mormon from the fantasy of his own mind would be folly. The audacity of such a lad, engaged in a fraudulent endeavor to deceive would surely have come to light if he had tried to include biblical scriptures in his record; and who could possibly have expected him to edit such venerable texts as Isaiah, Malachi, and the Sermon on the Mount.

It has been my desire in this study to show how perfect the Book of Mormon is. I have tried to show how remarkable it is that when there are translational differences between common texts, the Book of Mormon text is always the more clear; that the words come alive, and that difficult writings such as Isaiah's, hard for even his own people to understand, shed forth their beauty and their light from the pages of the Book of Mormon.

I have also tried to show the value of Old Testament prophecies and present reasons why they should appear in the Book of Mormon in the first place, and I have tried to show how those prophecies tie the one people to the other. As we read how difficult it was to write upon the gold plates, we should be in awe of the fact that men such as Nephi made the amazing effort to copy down words already recorded elsewhere. Even more remarkable is the fact that Mormon, as the abridger and compiler of that record, understood Nephi's motivation and agreed with him, so much so that even though he says he could not write even a hundredth part of all the records, he still stayed true to Nephi and included the words of Isaiah.

The Book of Mormon is a true and authentic book. Anyone who seeks to know this can find that same testimony by following Moroni's promise as found in Moroni 10:3–5. The knowledge of the truth comes from one source only and that source is the Holy Ghost. It is not my intention to convert anyone to the truthfulness of this book by intellect or persuasive argument. It is my intent, however, to show that, if it is a true book, then everything within its pages is there because Mormon thought it was important and it has a message of great worth for us. It is my humble desire that by learning the things in these pages the reader will come to esteem as of greater value, parts of the book which have, in the past, tended to be ignored.

> And now, if there are faults they are the mistakes of men; where-fore, condemn not the things of God, that ye may be found spotless at the judgment-seat of God.[2]

Notes

1. Roman soldiers were paid with salt, which gave rise to the common term *salary* from the Latin *sal,* or salt. In 1930 Mahatma Gandhi started with 78 followers and walked 241 miles across the Indian state of Gujarat in a march, ultimately joined by thousands, for the express purpose of scooping up a handful of salt from the historic coastal salt pans. This event, later called the "Salt March," ultimately led to the "Salt War" and the eventual ousting of Great Britain as the colonial ruler of India.
2. Title page, Book of Mormon

ABOUT THE AUTHOR

Mark Swint has been married for thirty-five years to his wife, Peggy Jo Wright. They have four children and four grandchildren with one more on the way.

Mark has spent his entire career pursuing his love of flying and is now a captain for a major airline flying international routes. His flying has given Mark the opportunity to share the gospel with people all over the world.

Mark's other passions are studying the scriptures and doing missionary work. Mark served a full-time mission in the Argentina South mission. He also served in the mission presidency of the Florida South mission, where he assisted with the work in Haiti, Jamaica, the Bahamas, and the Cayman Islands. He served as a Seventy on both ward and stake levels, a stake mission president, and on the high council over the stake mission. He has spent the rest of his time teaching the gospel in various classes. He presently serves as the Sunday School president for the Paseo Verde Ward of the Henderson Nevada Anthem Stake.

Mark wrote this book for his youngest son, Daniel, as he prepared for his mission to Peru. His intent was to show that every part of the Book of Mormon was valuable and filled with great truths.

Visit Mark's website, www.markswint.com, to learn more.

0 26575 09608 8